RADICALS AND CONSERVATIVES

RADICALS
AND
CONSERVATIVES

William Montgomery McGovern
and
David S. Collier

HENRY REGNERY COMPANY
1957

Contents

RADICALS AND CONSERVATIVES

[I]

Liberalism: A Twofold Tradition

THE MEANING OF LIBERALISM

IN THE PREAMBLE to the North Atlantic Treaty, the British and American governments, along with the other signatory members, solemnly affirm that "they are determined to safeguard the freedom, common heritage, and the civilization of their peoples, founded on the principles of democracy, individual liberty and the rule of law." This statement, especially the words "principles of democracy" and "individual liberty," are of great significance.

Adherence to the principles of democracy and individual liberty has played a major role in political developments from the time of the Reformation and Counter Reformation. It was belief in democracy and individual liberty which brought about the expulsion of the Stuarts in England and led to the American and French revolutions. During the nineteenth century most of the governments of Western Europe were changed in such a way as to make them conform to some extent with these two principles; and during the same period all governments established in the New World were based,

in name at least, upon them. During the twentieth century most of the new constitutions constructed for the
governments of Asia and Africa have also been based
upon a frank acceptance of democracy and individualism. It is only in countries with totalitarian regimes
that the two principles are rejected.

It is evident, therefore, that belief in democracy and
individualism is the basis of a widespread and powerful
political movement and the core of a widespread and
dynamic political philosophy. It is thus rather astonish-
ing to find it difficult to give a name to the philosophy
and movement as a whole. The fact that it has been
given different names at different times and places
makes it essential that we agree on some one term.

For historical reasons, we shall apply the terms
"liberal" and "liberalism" to those political movements
and ideologies based upon an adherence to the two principles of democracy and individualism.

Before going further, however, we must distinguish
our concept of liberalism from other concepts with
which the term has at times been associated.

At some times and places, especially in the United
States in recent years, the word "liberalism" has been
used to denote left-wing radicalism. Not infrequently
it implies a tinge of socialism or even of Communism.
As a result many persons think of liberals as "fellow
travellers" on the bandwagon of Kremlin ideology. It
should be clearly and definitely stated that we do *not*
attach this significance to the term "liberal." We feel
justified in refusing to associate liberalism with any and
every form of socialism, because liberalism at most
times and places has stood in sharp contrast with socialism. On the continent of Europe the word "liberalism"
has long meant and still means primarily a belief in
individualism in general, and in some form of free

private enterprise in particular. Most liberals, to be sure, do not accept a rigid system of laissez faire; but, historically speaking, due regard for individual rights, even in the economic sphere, has always played an integral part in the European concept of the liberal tradition. In Australia, in New Zealand, and in Japan the so-called Liberal parties are the principal opponents of socialism, and even in England the Liberals have refused to coalesce with the Labor party on the grounds that the latter is excessively imbued with socialistic ideology.

At some times and places the words "liberal" and "liberalism" have been associated primarily with a desire for change and innovation. Such a conception is due in large measure to the fact that in England for many decades the Liberal party, which advocated marked changes in political and social life, was opposed to the Conservative party, which was supposed to believe in holding fast to traditional ideas and to long-standing forms of government. This identification of liberalism with a desire for change is highly distorted and historically inaccurate. Many liberals have wanted change, but for the most part they wanted change only in a certain direction, not change merely for the sake of change. In many cases, moreover, outstanding liberal leaders have demanded the retention of old institutions which they regarded as good and have rejected proposed innovations which they regarded as bad; and in not a few cases important liberal leaders have demanded that the state revert to earlier forms of government. When the existing regime is dominated by autocracy or despotism, the followers of the liberal tradition are ardent reformers and demand widespread political changes. When, on the other hand, a country has a free and democratic government and this government seems threatened by a trend towards autocracy and despotism, the true liberal is conservative, resisting all efforts to overthrow the existing regime. This is true at the present time; it has also been true in the past.

In eighteenth-century France, when absolutism was the rule, the French liberals were advocates of change, of reform—even of revolution. But in sixteenth- and seventeenth-century France, in which there were many traces of semi-democratic or at least of parliamentary rule despite the marked trend towards absolutism, the outstanding French liberals—men such as François Hotman—insisted that the country should abide "by the good old ways" and refuse to embark upon political changes. It is universally agreed that Montesquieu and Burke because of their crusade against tyranny and arbitrary rule were preeminent exponents of liberalism; yet both men were essentially conservative in outlook. In the twentieth century the Italian and German liberals adamantly opposed the innovations which led to Fascism and Nazi-ism; and today true liberals adamantly oppose innovations which might lead to a totalitarian regime modeled after that of Moscow.

At some times and places, especially in southern Europe and in Latin America during the nineteenth and twentieth centuries, there has been a tendency to confuse liberalism with secularism or anti-clericalism. It is true that many of the outstanding leaders of liberal opinion in France, in Italy, and in South America have been violently against ecclesiastical interference in political affairs, and not a few have been agnostics or even atheists; but to identify liberalism, in the broad sense of the word, with irreligion is an absurdity. Many of the foremost exponents of liberal doctrines have been Jesuit and Calvinist theologians. Burke, Gladstone, and Lord

Acton were not professional theologians to be sure; but they were all ardent Christians, and their piety in no way interfered with their advocacy of liberal principles, but rather tended to strengthen it. The MRP party in France and the Christian Democratic party in Italy, which play important roles in contemporary politics, are frank defenders of Christian dogma and of the Catholic church; but both parties by their advocacy of democracy and individual rights are firmly within the boundaries of liberal tradition.

DEMOCRACY AND INDIVIDUALISM

Liberalism in the broad sense of the term means for us a political movement or a political philosophy which, on the one hand, advocates democracy as opposed to authoritarianism (the rule of the one or few) and, on the other, advocates individualism as opposed to statism (the rule of the all powerful state). Conversely, the antithesis of liberalism, which is totalitarianism, compounds within itself these two elements of authoritarianism and statism as direct opposites of democracy and individualism. At this point it is essential to bear in mind that, though in modern times democracy and individualism have often been closely associated, there exists a fundamental difference between the two, and liberalism is true to its historical heritage only so long as it remains a staunch defender of *both* ideas.

Democracy means, of course, that all sections and classes shall have a voice in the establishment and control of the organs of government, but there are many types and degrees of democracy. In some countries democracy implies the right of all adults, male or female, to vote and to be elected to office. In other countries women are ruled out and democracy means merely universal manhood suffrage. Elsewhere the right to vote or hold office is limited by property or literacy tests. Nevertheless, a regime must be called democratic if ultimate control over the machinery of government rests with the bulk of the people rather than with a special minority.

Individualism, in sharp contrast to democracy, implies the right of each person to control his own life so long as he does not seriously interfere with the liberty of others. It asserts the right of each person to "life, liberty, and the pursuit of happiness." Individualism is intimately associated with the concept of freedom: it demands freedom of thought, of speech, and of writing within the widest possible range. Individualism implies that every person possesses certain basic rights in the economic sphere, such as the right to choose his occupation or profession without governmental interference. Individualism implies a belief in and respect for private property—the right of each person to control his own belongings so long as his control does not seriously interfere with the economic welfare of his fellow citizens.

There are different types and degrees of individualism, just as there are different types and degrees of democracy. Practically all individualists believe in far-reaching freedom of thought and expression, but even professed individualists differ widely as to the amount of freedom of action which the state should grant to each citizen. Many individualists maintain that freedom of action means that a man should be permitted to perform any act, even an act contrary to the moral code of the community, so long as his act inflicts no harm on other persons. Others, claiming that liberty does not imply license, look to the state to punish acts patently contrary to moral law. Many individualists are convinced that true individualism implies laissez faire. Others insist that true individualism not only permits but requires a certain amount of governmental regulation of economic and industrial life, on the ground that under the system of laissez faire the average man comes under the control of monopolistic capital enterprise and hence ceases to have real freedom of action.

But though there are marked differences of opinion concerning the exact meaning and scope of individualism, all persons who claim to be individualists are agreed on their ultimate ideal, however much they may disagree on the means of securing it. This ultimate ideal is the greatest possible real freedom for each individual. To the individualist the state must be regarded not as an end in itself, but merely as a means to an end, and in consequence it seems to him completely wrong for the individual to be subordinated to or in any way sacrificed for the state.

Many persons, especially Englishmen and Americans, tend to co-identify democracy and individualism. They take it for granted that democracy necessarily implies a respect for individual rights and that individualism necessarily fosters the growth of democracy. Closer examination shows very clearly that though the two doctrines are not incompatible they are quite separate and distinct, and the acceptance of the one does not inevitably mean the acceptance of the other. History shows that it is quite possible to have a state in which the governmental machinery is in the hands of a single person, even a hereditary monarch, but in which a large measure of freedom of thought, of expression, and of action are granted the individual citizen. Such a state is simul-

taneously autocratic and individualistic in character.
Thus, while Prussia at the time of Frederick the Great
and China under the Manchu emperors had thoroughly
autocratic governments, the people of both countries en-
joyed a very large measure of freedom in the conduct
of their private lives.

It is also quite possible to have a thoroughly democratic regime which ignores the doctrines and the claims
of individualism. Democracy is essentially majority
rule, and individualism asserts that even the majority
has no right to demand complete domination over the
actions of minority groups, or of even a single individual.
In a country which is overwhelmingly of one religious
faith, a popularly elected assembly might well pass a
law forcing all citizens to join the church of that faith;
or a country in which the majority of citizens were non-
smokers might through a popular referendum pass a
law prohibiting the use of tobacco by all persons. Such
laws would be democratic, but in direct opposition to
the principles of individualism.

As a matter of fact, democracy is frequently associated not with individualism but with totalitarianism.
For a considerable time, apparently, a large majority
of Germans actively supported Hitler, and an even
larger percentage of Japanese actively supported Tojo.
Both regimes could thus claim to be "democratic," even
though both were clearly totalitarian. In like manner the
Communist party, in name at least, accepts the principles and uses the name of democracy while openly supporting not individualism but statism and totalitarianism.

Despite the possibility of divorcing democracy and
individualism, there has been for several centuries a
steady stream of political thinkers who have made it

their lifework to champion both. To these thinkers we give the title of liberals, if only because that was the name so many of them gave to themselves.

RADICALS AND CONSERVATIVES

Liberalism, according to our definition, means then the acceptance of both democracy and individualism as the basic doctrines in a political creed, but even within the compass of this definition there are many different types of liberals, some of them with violently opposed ideas. Both Burke and Bentham must be called liberals; yet we know that the followers of Burke and the followers of Bentham were frequently in sharp disagreement. We must grant the title of liberal both to the Federalists and the Whigs, on the one side, and to the followers of Jefferson and Jackson, on the other, in spite of the long and bitter antagonism between the two groups. To know the true meaning and significance of the liberal movement we must consider not only those points on which the various subgroups agreed, but also the points on which they disagreed.

Indeed, there was something unique about each of the great liberal leaders of the past several centuries. Each had his own personal philosophy, formed to an extent by the time, place, and conditions in which he lived; but even among political friends and associates of any one time and place there were frequently sharp divergences: Alexander Hamilton and John Adams, both Federalists, disagreed with each other on many important issues; between Jefferson and Jackson, ordinarily classed together, there was radical opposition on certain basic beliefs.

A comprehensive survey of the entire liberal movement, which would have to consider the political philosophy of at least a hundred eminent men, lies outside the scope of our present undertaking, which is to describe the general lines of development of the movement. This task is made easier by the fact that liberalism despite its diversity has from its very beginning, and especially from the middle of the eighteenth century, been generally divided into two main branches or subdivisions, which we may call, with some hesitation, radical liberalism and conservative liberalism.

Use of the two terms implies that not all liberals are radical. Perhaps less immediately apparent is the fact that not all radicals are liberal. A radical is one who admits of no compromise. He is single-minded, thoroughgoing, and extremist. In politics he wishes to make root-and-branch changes and reforms. He usually has a clear-cut scheme of how society and the nation should be organized, and every institution which is not in accord with his plan is to be ruthlessly swept aside. A radical demands that his changes or reforms be made immediately, and not piecemeal but all together. Not infrequently he insists that these reforms be carried out by force. He is usually convinced that if his scheme of life is carried out the result will be the opening of a golden age in which mankind will approach if not achieve perfection.

When Plato urged that all the existing political institutions of his time be discarded and the state be completely reorganized on a rational or "scientific" basis with all governmental powers concentrated in the hands of a few philosophers, he was a radical, though he was far from being a liberal. When the Fascists marched on Rome and demanded the immediate overthrow of the existing government and the establishment of an authoritarian regime, they were assuredly radical, though they were directly opposed to liberal principles. When the Communists demand the violent overthrow of the existing political and social order and the establishment of a totalitarian government controlled by a "dictatorship of the proletariat," they are undeniably radicals, but they are not liberals.

Nevertheless, during the past few centuries a number of important and able men have been both radical and liberal in their mode of thought and action. Thomas Jefferson, at least as a young man, and Jeremy Bentham, the great English reformer, are classical examples. Both were ardent supporters of democracy and individualism and were thus certainly liberals. But both men demanded the immediate and thoroughgoing application of democratic and individualistic principles to all men and to all nations. They also believed that the root-and-branch application of these principles would in itself bring about a regime in which all men are wise and good and prosperous. For these reasons they must also be called radicals. They were, in short, radical liberals. For purposes of brevity and convenience we shall call such men radicals. The reader should bear in mind that all of the so-called radicals with whom we deal in the present work kept well within the limits of the liberal tradition.

Among the radicals (or radical liberals) there have been profound differences of opinion at different times and places. During the eighteenth century most of the radicals centered their beliefs around the doctrines of natural law, natural rights, and the social contract. During the nineteenth century Bentham and his numerous followers rejected all of these doctrines and insisted that the sole basis of political action should be to secure "the greatest happiness of the greatest number."

Despite these differences, however, the radicals have

usually been in agreement about certain fundamental issues. First of all, they have emphasized a rather extreme form of democracy. They have insisted that thoroughgoing democratic principles are applicable at all times and places, irrespective of the previous cultural background of any particular people. They have ridiculed the idea that any nation, however backward culturally, has a need for a period of tutelage or preparation before it is capable of utilizing democratic institutions. Because of their devotion to democratic ideals the radicals have strenuously objected to the notion that any nation might retain a hereditary monarchy or a hereditary aristocracy in any form. They have also strenuously objected to any property qualification for voting or holding office. In the eighteenth century and the early part of the nineteenth, they demanded universal manhood suffrage. Since the middle of the nineteenth century most of them have been warm advocates of female suffrage as well. In recent years they have generally been in favor of lowering the age at which a person is qualified to vote.

In their devotion to extreme principles the radicals have tended to oppose the doctrine of judicial review—the idea that "a few old men" sitting as judges in a court of law can thwart the wishes of the majority of the citizens. Meaning by the "majority" a simple majority of 51 per cent of the general populace at any given time, the radicals have objected to the provisions of such charters as the American Constitution which require a special majority of two-thirds or three-quarters for changes in certain basic laws. The radicals have been in favor of direct as opposed to indirect democracy and have thus been against the indirect election of such officials as Senators or the President. Arguing that "the people" should decide not merely upon men but also upon issues, they have urged members of Parliament or Congress to reflect the views of the electorate rather than to vote in accordance with their own judgment, and have frequently advocated such institutions as the Initiative and Referendum as means whereby the general populace could directly influence legislation.

The radicals have insisted of course that democracy is the ideal form of government, and it has been difficult for them to admit that democratic government has any weaknesses or defects. They are convinced that any apparent failure of the democratic process may be cured by the establishment of a more radical form of democracy. During the eighteenth century most radicals believed that the actions of a democracy should be in accord with the dictates of "natural law" or divine law. During the nineteenth and twentieth centuries this belief has waned, and now most radicals tend to believe either that "the voice of the people (i. e., the majority) is itself the will of God," or else that there are no objective standards of value higher than the will of the majority.

In addition to standing for extreme democracy, the radicals have also been earnest and ardent advocates of thoroughgoing individualism; but there are sharp and very important differences between the individualism espoused by the radicals before the middle of the nineteenth century and the individualism recommended by them since.

The individualism of the earlier radicals was not only thoroughgoing, it was also consistently applied to all spheres of human activity, intellectual, moral, or economic. Believing the only function of the state to be the repelling of foreign invaders and the punishment of domestic crimes, the earlier radicals held that as long as a man did not commit a crime (defined primarily as the injury of others) he should be free to think, to say, and to do as he pleased. They believed, of course, in absolute liberty of thought and expression and contended that the state had no right to interfere with a man's religious or political opinions or to censor anything he might say or print. Most of the radicals also maintained that the individual should enjoy complete freedom in the moral sphere; that it was no part of the proper function of the state to enforce the moral code by legal sanctions. Finally, they believed that a man should be completely free in the economic sphere—free to buy and sell without being subject to state interference. He should have an absolute right to do as he pleases "with his own"—that is, with any property which legally belonged to him. Most of the early radicals, including Bentham, Jefferson, and Jackson, were enthusiastic advocates of laissez faire.

Since about 1850, and especially since 1880, there has been a sharp shift in the interpretation of individualism by the radicals. The later radicals continue to believe in absolute liberty of thought and expression. They continue to believe that the state has no right to punish a man for his religious, political, or economic opinions; and they extend this freedom from punishment not merely to the ordinary citizen but to elected and appointed officials, stigmatizing as acts of persecution even attempts to inquire into such opinions. Many of the modern radicals also continue to believe that a man should be free in the moral sphere, but a large number of them argue that a man is truly free only when he is willing and able to do what he *ought* to do. Contending that man is not free but a slave when he is addicted to such things as drinking, gambling, or sexually immoral acts, they assert that the state, in order to protect the "freedom" of the individual, should prohibit them.

Perhaps even more important has been the shift in the

ideas of the modern radicals on economic freedom. Whereas the older radicals believed passionately in the principle of a free market economy and insisted that the government should keep its hands off commerce and industry, the vast majority of the later radicals have gone to the other extreme and demand a very great measure of state regulation of all economic activity, since they feel that in a free economy the average private citizen falls under the domination of monopolistic enterprise and hence loses his freedom. Some of the more extreme radicals go so far as to say that "true freedom" is free enterprise in the life of the mind and that this can be achieved only when free enterprise in the economic sphere is completely abolished.

Turning now from the radicals (or radical liberals) to the conservative liberals, it is first necessary to emphasize the fact that not all conservatives are liberals. A conservative is one who wishes to preserve or conserve certain existing institutions or principles, and often these institutions and principles which the conservatives wish to preserve are in direct opposition to liberal ideas. Thus, during the eighteenth century those persons who wished to preserve absolute monarchy and the belief in the divine right of kings were conservatives, but they were not liberals. At the present time those Hindus who wish to preserve a rigid caste system are also conservatives, but they are far from being liberals. In like manner those persons who wish to preserve the Communist dictatorship which now exists in many of the countries of eastern Europe are conservatives, but they are certainly not acting in acord with liberal principles.

Nevertheless, during the past few centuries we have seen the rise of a number of great statesmen and political thinkers who were both conservative and liberal, and whom we can best describe as conservative liberals, though for purpose of brevity and convenience we shall call them merely conservatives, as we are concerned only with those conservatives who kept well within the limits of the liberal tradition. Among the outstanding conservatives (or conservative liberals) were the Frenchman Montesquieu, the Englishman Edmund Burke, and the American John Adams, though there are hundreds of others worthy of note.

There have, of course, been profound differences of opinion among the various conservative thinkers, but they have generally agreed on certain basic principles of political philosophy. They have always been skeptical of the idea that there is any single clear-cut scheme which will solve all of man's political, social, and economic difficulties. Though many of them have been ardent reformers, they have refused to believe that human nature can be completely transformed by legislation or that any set of political reforms will bring about the creation of a golden age.

The conservatives have always claimed to be great admirers of reason, but they have rejected all political schemes based solely upon abstract reason without reference to concrete experience and the accumulated wisdom of many generations. They have insisted that any one generation of men can progress only if it is willing and able to profit from the mistakes and successes of past generations and to make use of the stored-up practical wisdom of its ancestors. For this reason they insist that a society can be progressive only if it conserves its traditions.

The conservatives have consistently opposed the absolute rule of any one man, whether he be an hereditary monarch or a self-appointed dictator, and they have consistently defended representative government. Hence they must be called advocates of democracy; but they have not been extreme in their support of abstract democratic theories. They have argued that to be successful any system of government must be in accord with the spirit, the ideals, and the traditions of a people, and that consequently democratic institutions will work only if the nation adopting them has reached a cultural level at which its citizens are willing and able to shoulder the duties and responsibilities involved. The conservatives hold that, though democracy is the highest form of government, it is not necessarily suitable for immediate adoption at all times and places. When a people has had no experience with a democratic form of government it is better to let democracy develop slowly rather than to force its complete adoption at one fell blow.

According to the conservatives, democracy, even among peoples who have proved themselves capable of making it a success, has its weaknesses and limitations like all other forms of government, and these must be carefully guarded against. A well-established democracy can cease to exist if a large number of citizens become disinterested in public affairs and fail to vote, or if they become apathetic in the presence of bribery and corruption and the assumption of power by irresponsible political machines. Many conservatives have devised schemes to overcome some of these weaknesses and limitations of democracy, though the conservatives have not always been in agreement as to which plans are to be preferred.

Though nearly all of the conservatives have professed allegiance to the principle of majority rule, many have been especially concerned with defending the rights of minorities. They have frequently argued that changes in the basic law of the land should not be made in accordance with the passing whim of a bare majority, but should receive the consent of a much larger percentage of the total population. In their fear of irresponsible mob rule many conservatives, especially those in the New World, have adopted such principles as check and balance and the separation of powers. Most conservatives have also argued that the actions of the majority (like the actions of any minority) should be subject to the dictates of "natural" or higher law.

The conservatives have always been devout believers in the general principle of individualism. To be sure, they have not been as thoroughgoing or as extreme in their application of this principle as the radicals, but on the whole they have been more consistent. They have argued in favor of very far-reaching freedom of thought and expression, but they have insisted that this freedom cannot be absolute or unconditional. They have argued that ordinarily the state should have no concern with a man's religious or political convictions, but that when a religious or a political group preaches doctrines or engages in practices which constitute a "clear and present danger" to public health, general morality, or law and order, they may and should be curbed by governmental action. In general the conservatives have adopted the principle that a heresy—any heresy—is to be tolerated, but that a conspiracy, organized or otherwise, against public law and order must be arrested with dispatch.

Most conservatives have argued strongly against the idea that because an action is "immoral" it necessarily should also be made illegal. They have vigorously opposed most of the "blue" laws brought in by the Puritans as examples of undesirable collective control of public morals. They have argued that it is foolish for the state to pass laws against dancing, card playing, or horse racing. They have opposed laws prohibiting the sale and consumption of alcoholic beverages. At the same time they have argued against the idea that the state has no concern whatever with the private lives of its citizens. They have insisted that the state has not only the right but the duty to interfere when public morality is seriously threatened—as by outbursts of juvenile delinquency or by organized crime seeking to promote large-scale prostitution or gambling.

With respect to individualism in the economic sphere the conservatives have been more consistent than the radicals. During the period when the radicals were preaching extreme laissez faire, most of the conservatives took a more moderate approach. They have always been in favor of the general principle of private property and of property rights, but they also believed that the state should take an active interest in the economic welfare of its citizens. It was the conservative Federalists who placed in the American Constitution the phrase making it the duty of the state to "promote the general welfare," and it was they who believed that the state should take steps to foster the growth of commerce and industry. It was not they, but the radical Jeffersonians and Jacksonians who argued that the state should not interfere with the natural flow of economic forces. In England, it was the conservatives led by Lord Shaftesbury who sponsored the "Factory Laws" which resulted in ameliorating the conditions of labor in industry, while the radicals led by Cobden and Bright opposed such legislation.

When the radicals during the latter part of the nineteenth century reversed themselves and turned from extreme economic individualism toward economic collectivism, the conservatives tended, on the whole, to maintain their old position. While some of them were converted to laissez faire in view of the new threat of socialization, most of them continued to say that some control and regulation of industry were necessary; but at the same time they emphasized that the basic pattern of individual enterprise and individual property rights should not be forgotten, and they warned that complete socialization would be even more disastrous to the community than extreme economic individualism.

LIBERALISM : PAST AND PRESENT

Liberalism, despite its double emphasis on democracy and individualism and despite its division into radical and conservative wings, is nonetheless a single movement and political philosophy, within a single historical tradition. It is necessary to insist on this point, since during its historical development, so many particular brands of liberalism have claimed to be the only true kind and so many ideologies, actually anti-liberal in character, have attempted to gain acceptance by calling themselves liberal. The only way that liberalism can be restored to its former strength both as political movement and as political philosophy is to purge it of the confusions and false claims that have grown up around it.

The unity of liberalism can perhaps best be seen in the circumstances of its historical appearance at the close of the Reformation. Before this time, to be sure, a kind of proto-liberalism had at times been in existence: both in Periclean Athens and in Republican Rome we find many persons advocating democratic rule and demanding special consideration for the rights of individual citizens; and even during the Middle Ages democratic and individualistic doctrines were far from unknown. But liberalism in its modern form first found concrete expression just after the Reformation, when the nation-state first became the basic unit of political organization. Viewed narrowly, liberalism is simply an attempt to establish a proper form of government for the nation-state and to determine the relationship of that government to the individual citizen.

During the early part of the sixteenth century, it appeared for a time that authoritarianism, or totalitarian statism, would become the form of government adopted by the nation-state. Most of the nation-states were headed by hereditary monarchs who tended to secure absolute power over their subjects. The doctrine of divine right of kings received widespread acceptance, and by virtue of this doctrine the nation-states claimed, for the first time, the right to exercise complete control over all persons and groups of persons within their boundaries. It was in protest against the granting of absolute power to monarchs that there arose a number of thinkers and writers who proclaimed that on certain matters the state had no right to interfere with the thoughts, expressions, and actions of its citizens, and that the citizens themselves had the right to determine the extent of the authority of the state. These thinkers and writers were the first modern liberals.

After a near-century-long struggle, the liberal movement triumphed in England with the Glorious Revolution of 1688, with results that were to be far-reaching. With the deposition of James II, the principles that royal power should be limited, and that the people should have a voice in governmental affairs, were firmly established in England; and sharp limits were henceforth placed on the power of the state to interfere in the private life of its citizens. John Locke, the semi-official spokesman for the new revolutionary regime, was destined to dominate political thought for another century, not only in England but also in England's North American colonies and in France, which were the next two areas to put principles of liberalism into practical operation.

During the sixteenth and seventeenth centuries, before liberalism had been anywhere successful, there were many different phases in the liberal movement and many differences of opinion with regard to the particular application of its principles; but so long as liberalism as a whole faced a common enemy, divisions among liberals tended to be glossed over. With the downfall of absolute monarchy in England, and the triumph of certain basic principles common to both radical and conservative liberals, the inherent differences between the two groups came into the open and resulted in the emergence of two quite separate types of political philosophy.

Curiously enough, the first open conflict between these two types of thought came not in England but in France, about the middle of the eighteenth century, as a presage of the French Revolution. The *philosophes,* led by Voltaire, laid the foundations of what later became radicalism (or radical liberalism), and shortly thereafter radicalism received a new and rather different expression in the writings of Rousseau. Montesquieu outlined the basic ideas of what later emerged as conservatism (or conservative liberalism). These differences were soon reflected in England and in her North American colonies. In England the conservative point of view was expounded in various fashion by a line of thinkers ranging in time from Edmund Burke to Herbert Spencer, while radicalism was espoused by another group of political philosophers from Jeremy Bentham to T. H. Green. In America radicalism was most clearly expressed in the Declaration of Independence of 1776, while conservative thought dominated the writing of the Constitution of 1789. In both countries radicalism and conservatism received embodiment in competing political parties, whose immediate power struggles disguised the common ground of their basic convictions, and eventually gave the liberal movement as a whole the appearance not of unity but of two disparate groups ranged in irreconcilable opposition.

By the mid-twentieth century, conflicts within the liberal movement, confusions with regard to its basic meaning, and the false claims of rival ideologies to be "liberal" had so discredited the term "liberalism" that it was virtually without power. Part of this discredit had arisen from a tendency on the part of liberals to identify liberalism, not with its basic principles of democracy and individualism, but with its particular manifestations. In carrying out their internecine warfare, radical liberals and conservative liberals alike had attempted to apply the qualifying adjectives to their opponents and to reserve the noun for themselves. Radical liberals saw themselves as "liberals" opposed by "conservatives"; conservative liberals, at least in the United States until recent years, shunned the title "conservative" for themselves, but did not hesitate to label their radical liberal opponents simply as "radical."

Similarly, whenever political movements in other countries of the world resulted in either the overthrow of hereditary monarchs, the establishment of the trappings of parliamentary democracy, or even the formation of new nation-states, liberals in England, the United States of America, and France greeted these developments as milestones on the road toward the inevitable triumph of liberalism. They hailed as ends what in their own histories had been only means to the real goal of achieving the best possible combination of democracy and individualism. It is not going too far to say that the expenditure of blood and treasure exacted from the older liberal democracies during the first half of the twentieth century was the price they paid for their failure to understand at one and the same time their own basic principles and the meaning of political developments in Italy, Germany, Japan, and Russia.

The liberal democracies paid not only in terms of destruction of human life and economic value, but in debilitation of spirit. Forgetful that adherence to both democracy and individualism is essential for the continued vitality of liberalism, sincere but confused liberals allowed themselves to be led astray alternately by extreme individualists who did not believe in democracy, by extreme democrats who had no love for individualism, and by totalitarian statists who believed in neither but proclaimed their belief in both. Instead of symbolizing actual values, terms like "liberalism," "freedom," "democracy," and "individualism" became catchwords to attract a following to serve the ambitions of the unscrupulous. The inevitable disillusionment that followed such naive bestowal of faith ended by destroying faith itself.

Today, when a man proclaims himself to be a "liberal," one rightly tends to regard him with suspicion. Too often the coin accepted as sterling has turned out to be debased or counterfeit. Such being the case, is the effort to reestablish the term "liberal" worthwhile? Continuing the metaphor, we may reply by answering that the evil of a debased or counterfeit currency is not remedied by doing away with money, but by restoring its value. To be sure, it may be contended that the term "liberalism" in and of itself has no more value than money does. Both are symbols of value—valuable only in terms of what they refer to. Realization of the symbolic character of the term "liberalism" is, however, precisely what makes us define it in reference to the true value that it should express—a combined adherence to democracy and individualism.

At the risk of being repetitious, it is here necessary

to reemphasize our main point: liberalism, despite the dichotomy of its goal, and despite its division into two major divisions of thought and many subdivisions, expresses a single, unitary political movement and philosophy. That there is diversity in this unity is not a element of weakness but of strength. Indeed, whenever the diversity of liberalism is sacrificed in the name of unity, or its unity forgotten through overemphasis of its diversity, liberalism is weakened—even as it is weakened whenever one of its two basic goals, democracy and individualism, is stressed at the expense of the other.

In short, liberalism as a political philosophy is devoted to a proper balance between equally desirable opposing forces; and liberalism as a political movement is the process of determining that proper balance at any one time and place. "Proper balance" may be further defined, as we shall see later, as the realization of the greatest amount of freedom consistent with the well-being of the group in whose name political action is taken. Liberalism is thus not an unchanging body of rules applicable to all times and circumstances. Rather, liberalism is the expression of an attitude, the assertion of devotion to certain values, and in addition a guide by which those values may be possibly, but not inevitably, realized. Elaboration of the concept of liberalism, so regarded, is the purpose of the following chapters of this book.

In our brief discussion of the liberal thinkers of the past, there was one political philosopher whose name we omitted—John Stuart Mill. The omission was deliberate, since alone among the liberal writers of the past, Mill belongs clearly to neither the radical nor conservative wings of the liberalism. Mill's significance lies in the fact that he was the last of the great liberal political philosophers to attempt to reconcile the widening dif-

ferences between radical and conservative liberals; and
for that reason his thinking is of unusual importance for
the exposition that lies ahead. In the pages that follow
we shall refer to Mill many times, sometimes in agreement and sometimes in disagreement. Indeed, we shall
make a critical analysis of the major aspects in the
thought of most of the great liberal political philosophers, both radical and conservative, accepting or dis-
carding elements of their thinking in accordance with
the light that subsequent history and scientific knowledge provides.

We must confess, however, that while many of the
tenets of the radicals are accepted by us, more often than
not it is the conservatives rather than the radicals whom
we find getting the best of the argument. Indeed, it is
our hope that we shall be able to provide at least the
beginnings of a coherent philosophy of conservative
liberalism. Historical circumstance, in addition to personal conviction, leads us to this task. If during the latter
half of the nineteenth century, liberalism perhaps over-
emphasized individualism at the expense of democracy,
during the first half of the twentieth an unqualified
devotion to democracy, real and imagined, has threatened the extinction of individual freedom. The very
character of liberalism as the expression of a proper
balance demands a reemphasis of individualism. If we
go further and indicate that a proper balance, regardless
of the time and circumstance, is usually found at a point
a little to the right of center, it is because conservative
liberalism has a concern for the preservation of past
value which radical liberalism does not. Upon the continuance of such a concern depends the fate of liberalism
as a whole.

In addition, as we shall see in the following chapter,
there are signs that the twentieth-century swing toward

collectivism—at its best an overstressing of the democratic element in the liberal tradition, and at its worst an outright devotion to a new authoritarianism—has run its course. The most vital political movement in the world today realizes itself as anti-collectivism, but it fails to understand that it is expressing in action—albeit in rather bumbling fashion—the political philosophy of conservative liberalism. Clear statement of this political philosophy, so that it may strengthen the anti-collectivist movement by serving as its guide, is thus no mere exercise in theory, but a work of immense practical importance; for on the success of the anti-collectivist movement depends the hope of men for balanced freedom in our time and in the future.

[2]

Collectivists and Anti-Collectivists

THE REPUDIATION OF COLLECTIVISM

DURING THE FIRST HALF of the twentieth century it appeared as though nearly all the countries of the world were marching steadily towards some sort of collectivism. Among radical liberals this movement took the form of an excessive emphasis on democracy at the expense of individualism; while radicals outside the liberal tradition, who had no belief in either democracy or individualism but often pretended to, turned to some variety of totalitarianism. Whether espoused by radical liberals or totalitarians, collectivism invariably introduced a state control of economic affairs, with an inevitable tendency toward state control in non-economic matters as well. Democratic collectivists, of course, differed with totalitarian collectivists as to the nature and number of controls to be introduced; and they proclaimed their intention of stopping far short of a complete state authoritarianism. It was clearly demonstrated, however, by the course of the collectivist movement that such a stopping-short was well-nigh impossible.

The swing toward collectivism was felt not only in the new nation-states but in the old liberal democracies as well. In England, in Australia, and in New Zealand, Labor parties were formed and became increasingly powerful, and in all cases these parties pledged themselves to carry out a full program of socialization. In 1917, after a brief experiment with socialism, Russia fell into the hands of the Communists, who proceeded to apply the Marxist form of collectivism by brute force. In 1922 Italy fell under the control of the Fascists, who though bitterly anti-Communist adopted a special form of totalitarian collectivism.

The great world depression of the 1930's in a great many countries resulted in a rapid acceleration of the trend toward collectivism. A substantial majority of the inhabitants of these countries came to believe that individualism, at least in the economic sphere, led to mass misery and to feel that the general well-being of the community could be restored and maintained only if the state rigidly controlled and regulated all forms of commercial and industrial life. In the United States the trend took the form of the "New Deal" of Franklin D. Roosevelt and of the "Fair Deal" of Harry Truman. In Germany and Japan it took a much more militant and extreme form resulting in the triumph of National Socialism and militarism.

The results of World War II caused the forcible suppression of the Nazi-Fascist governments of Italy, Germany, and Japan, but greatly strengthened the Communist form of collectivism, which retained a firm hold upon the U.S.S.R. and in addition secured effective control over most of the countries of eastern Europe. In 1949 the Communist party extended its control over the whole mainland of China; and, contrary to the illusions of many so-called "liberals," the Chinese Communists proceeded to establish a totalitarian collectivist regime in a rigorous and ruthless manner, killing off millions of persons who ventured to oppose them.

In the British Empire and in America a much milder form of collectivism continued to triumph. In the English elections of 1945 the Conservatives were swept out of office, and the Laborites, put in charge of the government, promptly proceeded to nationalize several of the major British industries. In Australia and New Zealand the Labor party with its socialist program retained its power. In the United States, the victory of Harry Truman and his "Fair Deal" associates in the election of 1948 to many observers seemed to foretell the eventual triumph of complete collectivism in America.

Just at this time the tide began to turn. In many countries the people who had been forced to live under a collectivist or statist regime became increasingly restive. Many persons became convinced that socialism was not the panacea for all of a nation's woes or even for its economic ills. In most instances it was the middle classes who were foremost in revolting against the frustrations which accompanied programs entailing wholesale and thoroughgoing collectivism, but not infrequently it was the working men themselves (or their wives) who realized that nationalization of industry did not automatically make for higher wages and better living conditions. In Australia and New Zealand general elections resulted in the ousting of Labor governments and the establishment of the Liberal party, pledged to oppose the further spread of collectivism. In the English elections of 1950 the people rejected the Laborites and returned the Conservatives who promptly proceeded to denationalize a number of the industries taken over by the previous Labor government. That these measures did not meet with popular disapproval is shown by the fact that in 1955 the Conservatives received an even stronger mandate from the electorate.

In the American election of 1952 the Democrats were overwhelmingly defeated and a Republican elected President, although the issues were far from clear cut. Many persons voted for the Republican candidate because of his personal background; and many of the Democrats, especially those in the South, were as anti-collectivist as a majority of the Republicans. But it is certain that the Republican promise to restrain "creeping socialism" was a factor and an important one in deciding the election. The 1956 national contest reelecting by overwhelming majority the Republican incumbent, but failing by narrow margins to provide a Republican Congress, did not change the trend. Rather the President's high plurality and an examination of the issues on a candidate to candidate basis tended to reaffirm the general direction of popular feeling.

Of great interest was a similar shift in public opinion in Japan and Germany. For over a decade both countries had been subjected to statist regimes which consistently became more rigid until they culminated in totalitarian collectivism. The war swept away this type of government in both countries, but many observers were of the opinion that the Germans and the Japanese were so accustomed to the regimentation of their lives that they would be unable to tolerate the restoration of individualism in political and economic life. In both countries, moreover, many of the Occupation officials were themselves collectivists (though of the milk-and-watery socialist or "Fair Deal" type) and strove to maintain collectivism as an integral part of the regimes in the two countries under their control. It was soon clear, however, that the majority of both the German and the Japanese people, from their long experience of rigid regulation and control, had become disgusted with collectivism. When free elections were permitted, the Germans put into office Adenauer and his Christian Democrats, and the Japanese installed Yoshida and his *Jiyūto* or Liberals. The two regimes had much in common, including a dislike of extreme collectivism and a belief in some form of competition and free enterprise. (Incidentally the collectivists were considerably startled by the enormous success achieved by the Christian Democrats in their handling of economic affairs, which resulted in the amazing rehabilitation of German commerce and industry in marked contrast to the lagging efforts of countries, such as France, which maintained a large measure of collectivist control.)

It is quite possible that this shift in public opinion away from collectivism is only a temporary phenomenon, and that the tendency may be reversed during the course of the next few decades. On the other hand it is equally possible that collectivism, at least in its more extreme form, is permanently on the wane except where it is maintained by force. One strong reason for believing this is the fact that many persons, including many able intellectual leaders formerly in the forefront of the crusade for collectivism, have become disillusioned with many aspects of the collectivist philosophy.

Take, for example, Norman Thomas, for many years the distinguished leader of the Socialist party in America and on several occasions the Socialist candidate for the Presidency. Dr. Thomas is still a convinced collectivist, and he firmly denies that he has renounced the socialist creed; but in a work entitled *Democratic Socialism,* published in 1953, he frankly admits the weakness of many of the traditional collectivist assumptions and conclusions. He rejects the old collectivist assumption that human nature, apart from environmental differences, is everywhere uniform: "We are not all of one piece," he asserts. "And we do not act under any one incentive. . . . Men are bundles of many different qualities, motives, and aspirations."[1] He admits that selfishness and greed is to be found not only in the capitalist but also in the working class: "The Working Class is not the Messiah which some of us thought."[2] He also admits that "nationalization of industry in Great Britain and elsewhere has not been the simple solution of all problems which many socialists in their age of faith had assumed."[3] Studies of Fascist and Communist states "have sharpened our fears of the state as the master of human society," and even in democratic England and America experience "has made us more aware than formerly of the dangers of statism."[4] In the international sphere collectivism also has its limitations: "Socialism is not a panacea against war. . . . Socialists are not warranted in repeating the once popular statement that capitalism is the cause of war and that the only hope of peace is universal Socialism."[5]

Dr. Thomas wishes to strengthen the spirit of cooperation, but he frankly admits that "the spirit of emulation or competition is still deeply rooted in us. A completely non-competitive society would be dull and stagnant. . . . Socialism should try and stress competition for the laurel leaf rather than the sack of gold . . . but it should recognize that material progress has been furthered by competition for material reward."[6] Because of this fact, Dr. Thomas even acknowledges that an excessively heavy income tax may become "a threat to incentive."

[1] *Democratic Socialism*, p. 24.
[2] *Ibid.*, p. 38.
[3] *Ibid.*, p. 4.
[4] *Ibid.*, pp. 6-7.
[5] *Ibid.*, p. 14.
[6] *Ibid.*, p. 22.

He still wishes to place some of the large basic industries under government control, but he grants that an attempt to socialize all commerce and industry would be fatuous: "There are some advantages for freedom and enterprise in varieties of ownership. The state under the most democratic theory and practice will become too huge, too cumbersome if it seeks to control directly all economic activity. There are men with a deep seated desire to work for themselves. They will work harder and be more ingenious in so doing."[7]

In England we also find a number of collectivist intellectuals being forced to reconsider the assumptions and the conclusions which were accepted without question a generation or two ago. It is of interest to compare the original *Fabian Essays,* written in 1883 by the founders of the Fabian Socialist movement, with a book entitled *New Fabian Essays* written in 1951 by the present-day intellectual leaders of the Fabian Society. The authors of the original *Fabian Essays* (the Webbs, H. G. Wells, and others) were confident and dogmatic. They were certain that their assumptions regarding the nature of man and of society were valid; from these assumptions it was clear to them that the whole world was assured of a glorious future through the inevitable triumph of socialism throughout the world. Throughout the *New Fabian Essays,* on the other hand, there is a constant note of disillusionment and baffled hope. The authors are still devoted to the socialist cause, but they are frank to admit that many of the old socialist assumptions were fallacious and that many of the results of socialist legislation have not had the happy consequences which were expected.

R. H. S. Crossman, editor and one of the authors of

[7] *Ibid.,* p. 27.

the *New Fabian Essays,* pointing out that the original Fabian doctrine was based in large measure upon some assumptions derived from Bentham and others taken over from T. H. Green and the "Social Gospellers," admits that the grim events of recent times have shown that many of these assumptions can no longer be accepted as valid. He finds it necessary to reject Bentham's theories regarding the nature of man, accepted by most of the earlier Fabians, and also rejects Green's theory of constant and inevitable progress, which played such an important part in early Fabian thought. The notion of automatic progress is now seen to be an illusion. The present trend is not toward Fabian Socialism, which desires true equality and respect for individual personality, but towards ruthless totalitarianism which most Fabians regard with intense dislike.

It is clear that Mr. Crossman and many other present-day Fabians are rather disappointed by the results of the program of the nationalization of several basic industries carried out by the Labor government during its period in office. They claim that this nationalization of industry has had many beneficial results, but they admit that it has not been an unmixed blessing. It has not always brought about greater democracy and equality, for in many cases it has merely resulted in placing effective power in a small managerial class or civil service elite. The new Fabians are willing to state that in many cases nationalization of industry has resulted in greater inefficiency and a marked decrease in the production of goods badly needed by the general populace. For this reason it would appear that Mr. Crossman believes it not advisable for the Labor party to demand further nationalization of industry, at least for the time being. Other Laborite intellectuals do not agree with this point of view, but it is of interest to note that several of those persons who wish to press for further nationalization note that under the regime of socialized industry there has been a serious let-down in the spirit of thrift, diligence, and the desire to work. To such persons the only acceptable answer to this problem is for the state, by severe sanctions, to *compel* people to work harder and more efficiently. "The donkey needs to see the stick as well as the carrot."[8]

THE RISE OF CONSERVATIVE LIBERALISM

Since about 1950 in most countries outside of the Iron Curtain the collectivists have been forced from the offensive to the defensive, and in many cases the anti-collectivists have been able to win notable victories. What political philosophy lies behind these major anti-collectivist movements of the present day?

At first sight the question appears difficult if not impossible to answer with any accuracy, for the anti-collectivist movement has taken very different forms in different countries. The Republicans under Eisenhower, the Conservatives under Churchill, Eden, and Macmillan, the Christian Democrats under Adenauer, and the Liberals and Democrats of Japan under Yoshida, Hatoyama, Ishibashi, and Kishi, do not and can not have exactly the same beliefs and aspirations. Even within each country the anti-collectivists fall into several different categories. In England, for example, nearly all anti-collectivists feel called upon to support the Conservative party, but inside this party there are some persons who can be called "Tory Reactionaries" and others who can be called "Middle of the Roaders," who are opposed to out-and-out collectivism but who wish to

[8] Cf. the views of E. H. Carr, *The New Society,* and P. C. G. Walker, *Restatement of Liberty.*

retain a number of the features of the welfare state. The same or a similar situation exists in all the other countries where the anti-collectivists have come into political power.

Nevertheless, in spite of these national and intra-national differences, a comparative study of the concrete legislative programs makes it possible to characterize in a broad and general way the main tendencies of the anti-collectivist movements. In the first place, it is noteworthy that most of them are characterized by a marked spirit of moderation. They are opposed to both right-wing and left-wing extremism. Even in Germany and Japan the followers of Adenauer, of Yoshida, and his successors are as opposed to Fascism and Nazi-ism as they are to socialism and Communism. It goes without saying that the same situation is true with respect to the anti-collectivist movements in the English-speaking countries. Yet, though the various anti-collectivist movements are and necessarily must be opposed to socialism and statism, in no case have they demanded a return to radical or extreme individualism. They do insist that a healthy respect should be given to the general principles of competition, a free market economy, and private enterprise; but in all cases they insist, both in theory and in practice, that free competition works effectively only when it is tempered by the acceptance of certain moral and ethical standards ("fair play," "justice") by the bulk of the populace. When the abnormal activities of private business enterprises threaten the safety and welfare of the country as a whole, they must be checked; and, if necessary, such enterprises must be controlled and regulated by the state.

In most countries the anti-collectivist movement is called "conservative," but in many ways it would be more appropriate to call it both conservative and liberal, and to refer to the movement as conservative liberalism, just as we have done previously when examining it within its historical context. It is basically liberal because it pays deep respect both to democracy and individualism, because it tries to prevent both an overemphasis on democracy which might destroy individual freedom, and an overemphasis on individualism which might interfere with the proper working of democracy. It is certainly democratic because in none of the countries where the anti-collectivists have secured power has any attempt been made to limit the suffrage or to interfere with free popular elections. At the same time it is essentially individualistic, since it seeks to protect to the greatest possible extent the freedom of every person and groups within the state. In fact, it is this very respect for individualism which gives this movement its anti-collectivist bias.

The movement is thus liberal. But it is also conservative because it seeks to protect and preserve (or conserve) certain spiritual, moral, and ideological principles from the attack of extremists on both the right and the left. Among the principles which it seeks to conserve are, of course, the principles of democracy and individualism. The movement cannot rightfully be called reactionary, for, in no case has an attempt been made to re-establish the political, social, or economic conditions of the eighteenth or even of the nineteenth century. Conservative liberals realize that change of some sort is inevitable and that some changes, which we might better call "reforms," are eminently desirable. It will be remembered that many of the foremost "conservatives" of former times—men such as Montesquieu, Burke, and Adams—were also eminent reformers. It is equally true today that most of the persons who call themselves conservative believe that improvements in political, social, and economic conditions can and should be made. But today's conservatives also believe that reform and revolution are two different things; that revolution—an attempt to make a clean sweep of all existing institutions—is mostly disastrous, in many cases making it impossible to carry out badly needed reforms.

It is also clear that nearly all present-day conservative liberals are convinced that while some change is inevitable, not all change is progress; that some changes are to be welcomed and striven for, while others are to be shunned or resisted. The old idea that all change is progress and to resist any change is "unprogressive" is seen to be delusion, even as enlightened radicals such as Dr. Norman Thomas have discovered. For the democratic Germany of the Weimar constitution to give way to Nazi Germany was certainly change, but it can scarcely be called progress by anyone who believed in the democratic principle. In Czechoslovakia the shift from a reasonably free government to a totalitarian regime was certainly a change, but it would scarcely be called progress by anyone believing in the dignity and worth of the individual. In sum the modern conservative liberals assert that while change is constant and inevitable, progress is neither constant nor inevitable; that true progress is the application under various new conditions of certain basic ideals and principles which have proved their value and worth through generations of human experience.

[3]

Toward a Philosophy of Conservative Liberalism

THE LIMITATIONS OF SCIENCE

THE DEMOCRATIC anti-collectivist movement which we call conservative liberalism has achieved in recent years a widespread popularity in many different countries; but for the most part, it has been a practical movement and as yet has produced very few political philosophers. In fact, if the persons who support this movement were asked about their political philosophy, it is certain that most of them would give confused and widely divergent answers. Nevertheless, there has developed within the last few years a body of ideas and concepts which is in general accord with and gives support to the principles which guide most conservative liberal movements in their attempts to formulate concrete legislation. This body of ideas is not the creation of any one man or of any one group of men, and many of the men who have helped to develop it are in violent disagreement among themselves as regards details. But it may be of value and interest to attempt to describe in a general way this new type of political philosophy, which appears to be gaining acceptance in many different parts of the world.

Toward a Philosophy of Conservative Liberalism

We have spoken of this political philosophy as something new, although in numerous ways it is a synthesis of many old ideas, especially those of such men as Burke, the later Jefferson, and J. S. Mill. But it is also a synthesis which makes due allowance for recent advances in our knowledge of history and pre-history, and of similar advances in some of the natural and social sciences. Firmly within the liberal tradition, it is a body of thought which grows basically from the conservative wing, but it makes free use of the ideas formulated by many of the so-called radicals.

Any political theory to be sound must start with an examination of the problem of knowledge, or the problem of how much we can expect to know and how we can best achieve the knowable. Conservative liberals agree with the radical liberals that during most of the Middle Ages and even during the fifteenth and sixteenth centuries too great reliance was placed upon external authority as the major source of knowledge, whether this acceptance of authority took the form of a blind reliance upon tradition, or an equally uncritical reliance upon the ancient sages such as Aristotle, or upon certain passages in the sacred scriptures. But conservative liberals are equally insistent that during the seventeenth, eighteenth, and nineteenth centuries there was far too much emphasis placed upon abstract, a priori reasoning as the principal source of knowledge. Equally unfortunate were the results in which experience was supposedly involved but in which, in fact, basic premises were taken for granted without experimental check, and elaborate conclusions were then deduced from these premises. This type of reasoning weakened the political theories of Locke and of Bentham and thoroughly vitiated the political philosophies of Rousseau, of Hegel, and of Marx.

In general, we must accept the doctrine laid down by J. S. Mill and developed by many later thinkers that all *scientific* knowledge must be based upon a compound of experience and reason, or what is now commonly called the logico-experimental method. The ultimate source of most forms of knowledge is observation, or experience, and if possible experiment. But on the foundation of sense-data it is essential that we make use of our rational faculty to build up, inductively, some general conclusions. Once these conclusions have been further checked by experience, we can then make use of deductive reasoning or a combination of inductive and deductive reasoning to achieve further concepts, which again must be checked by experience. Sometimes, to be sure, we can begin by framing some rather startling premises which seemingly are not originated by sense experience (such as the premises of non-Euclidian geometry) and these can prove very valuable, but only when the conclusions deduced from these premises are checked by concrete observations and experiments. As far as *scientific* method is concerned, we must attempt to eliminate, as far as possible, all recourse to "intuition," tradition, or external authority. This rule applies not only to the physical sciences, but also to the social sciences, including the science of political behavior (or "political science").

So far, so good. Until the close of the nineteenth century most scientists optimistically believed that the logico-experimental method had already given us complete and accurate answers to many problems and might be expected eventually (with the further advance of science) to give complete and accurate answers to all questions, certainly to those concerning the material universe. In the early part of the twentieth century, however, certain rather amazing developments in physics, such as the formulation of the relativity and quantum theories, made even the natural scientists realize that there are now and probably always will be many marked limitations upon the applicability of the logico-experimental or scientific method. Indeed, the physicists themselves insisted that the logico-experimental method, though extremely valuable and irreplaceable, gives us an incomplete and in some ways an inadequate and even distorted picture of the external world. It is incomplete and inadequate because it gives us only a partial knowledge of reality; and because it is incomplete and inadequate, our understanding of this reality is necessarily distorted.

We have long known that the sense organs, though essential to us in our attempts to secure contact with external reality, are in many ways imperfect. We know, for example, that the human eye is a very valuable organ, but we also know that it is subject to many optical illusions. We also know that there are many things which remain invisible to the human eye (for example, infra-red and ultra-violet lights), although the existence of such things is definitely proved. The human eye, in fact, is what it is because of the long evolution which it has undergone. By a process of adaptation and by reason of the survival of the fittest, a type of eye has developed which sees sights and colors useful to the human organism, and which ignores sights and colors apparently more or less useless.

In like manner, reason or intellect, the faculty which human beings have developed during the course of evolution, is extremely valuable, but it too is subject to many limitations and is far from perfect. There are many phases of reality which the intellect is unable to grasp, and it is apt to give a distorted picture even of those phases which it is able to grasp. The picture it gives us is based upon the need for action rather than on a search for abstract truth. As long as the physical phenomena known to us were relatively simple, the human mind was able to cope with them more or less adequately, but with the enormous advance of physics in recent years the mind is forced to deal with phenomena which it has great difficulty in comprehending. In fact, it seems very probable that the ultimate reality which lies at the back of the phenomenal world follows a non-rational pattern, at least to the extent that it does not allow itself to be comprehended by the ordinary processes of reason or logic.

If the statements of science—the results of the logico-empirical method—though of supreme importance within their own field of application, are yet incapable of giving us a complete picture of reality, it is not surprising that most persons, including a great many scientists, try to supplement the results of science with concepts derived from other sources. "We are no longer taught that the scientific method of approach is the only valid method of acquiring knowledge about reality. Eminent men of science are insisting, with what seems a strange enthusiasm, on the fact that science gives but a partial knowledge of reality and we are no longer required to consider as illusory everything which science finds itself able to ignore. . . . We are no longer required to believe that our response to beauty, or the mystic sense of communion with God have no objective counterpart. It is perfectly possible that they are what they have so often been taken to be, clues to the nature of reality."[1]

Emphasis should be laid upon the phrase "clues to reality" for it is clear that non-logico-empirical methods, like the logico-empirical method itself, are unable to

[1] Sullivan, *Limitations of Science,* pp. 138, 142.

give a complete or adequate understanding of ultimate reality. Nevertheless, it would appear that in certain circumstances the results of the logico-empirical method can be rectified and supplemented by using other methods of approach. One of the methods most commonly used has been to pay some attention to what "intuition," "instinctive awareness," or "direct insight" can teach us—a method which must be practiced with great caution, because improperly employed it can lead to fantastic dogmas. Nearly everyone, however, including most scientists, makes use of this method at least to a limited extent. Even J. S. Mill, who usually went out of his way to deny "intuition" or innate feelings, was forced to admit that our belief in free will—to him a necessary belief—is "not based upon any process of logical argumentation, but upon immediate or spontaneous sense or some movement of consciousness." Mill admitted that according to the scientific concepts of his time, free will was absurd and he could think of no logical arguments against determinism, but on this point he felt it was necessary to accept the dictates of "intuition" rather than the doctrines of science: "It appears to me that every reasonable act of every sane man is a practical assertion of the existence of individual freedom."[2]

Apparently some form of "intuition" or "innate feeling" is an essential part of every value judgment. Every time a man says or thinks that something is good or bad, beautiful or ugly, some form of intuitive activity is involved. The same is true when a man says or thinks that he ought or ought not to perform some act. Nearly all scholars are agreed that the strict logico-empirical method is of little or no aid in forming value judgments. In most instances, science can give an accurate descrip-

[2] J. S. Mill, *Social Freedom,* pp. 32, 33. Cf. also B. Willey, *The 17th Century Background,* p. 114.

tion of what is happening; in many instances it can tell us what did happen in the past; in some instances it can tell us what will happen (or probably happen) in the future; but in no case can it tell us whether the events or the actions should be judged good or bad. And yet it is a fact that almost all persons do have value judgments. It is true that these judgments vary from person to person and considerably from nation to nation, showing that the *content* of the value judgments are greatly influenced by environment or upbringing. Nevertheless, the fact that there is a "feeling" of good and bad, beautiful and ugly, would appear to be due to an innate "instinct" or "intuition" in mankind, and due account must be taken of it in any system of political philosophy.

TRADITION

It is evident that "intuition" in some form or other is a factor of such importance in human life that it cannot be ignored. The same thing is true of tradition in its various forms. It is certainly true that there are good and bad traditions. Some are merely the results of ignorance, superstition, or the working of selfish interests; some have hindered the advancement of scientific knowledge; and others have aided in the spread of what we now call immoral or inhuman practices. But recent history shows that tradition has a good as well as a bad side. We have seen in the course of the last two centuries that when a nation has deliberately swept aside all traditional views and values, and tried to remake the world on a strictly "rational" basis, the results have always been calamitous both to the nation as a whole and to its component parts. In some cases tradition is merely accumulated ignorance, but in many other cases it is the accumulated wisdom of the ages. Tradition has frequently, though not invariably, been wrong when it usurped the role of science and attempted to give a detailed explanation of the material universe; but it has also frequently been right in its attitude towards human nature and in its appeal to forces which motivate human nature.

Tradition may be regarded in some ways as the result of the operation of intuition and of "unconscious reason" through the ages. Often this "unconscious reason" has proved itself of greater value than the operation of conscious reason at any one time and place, especially when both types of reason attempt to deal with human relationships. Even in the purely conceptual field, the very fact that a doctrine has been accepted by many generations of mankind or by a substantial portion of mankind is an important phenomenon which must be taken into account. The traditional doctrine may be found to be an inadequate or distorted variation of some basic truth; and even when this is not the case, we usually find that the doctrine was developed in order to satisfy some deeply felt want of human nature. Merely to ignore or to deny traditional doctrine would be ridiculous if one is trying to establish a satisfactory and comprehensive *political* philosophy.

Where value judgments are concerned, the role of tradition has proved even more important. We may well believe that neither the traditional Islamic nor Confucian moral codes was perfect or "scientific," but it is undoubtedly true that in historic times the widespread and wholehearted acceptance of these codes in the Near East and in China respectively resulted in modifying and weakening the tyranny of the Caliphs and Emperors, who in theory were the absolute masters of their subjects.

It is generally agreed that while the moral impulse

(the feeling that there is a good and a bad) is rooted in "intuition," the content of the so-called conscience is largely based upon tradition—the moral ideas of one's family, or community, or sect. In the eighteenth and nineteenth centuries many of the radical philosophers were violently opposed to tradition in any form as being merely blind allegiance to the barbarous past. Opposed to conventional or traditional morality merely because it was traditional, not infrequently such philosophers tried to formulate a rational or scientific system of ethics. Bentham, for example, tried to establish a moral code based exclusively upon hedonism and rational self-interest. His attempt was interesting, but must be considered a failure. Nearly all of the later Utilitarians who followed him felt forced to depart from his rigid system and so modify it as to conform in a general way with traditional moral concepts.

In the middle of the nineteenth century, when Darwinism became popular, some philosophers thought it necessary to establish a new system of ethics based upon the frank recognition that evolution and progress resulted solely from the struggle for existence and the survival of the fittest. This resulted in the "tooth and claw" philosophy—each man for himself, and destruction and death for the less fit. A decade or two later it was seen even by biologists that the acceptance of Darwinism did *not* require such an ethic. It was recognized that even on Darwinian principles evolution could not have taken place without a certain amount of altruism, cooperation, and benevolence between the members of a group struggling for existence. Fuller knowledge of the process of evolution, instead of destroying traditional morality, gave added strength to many of its concepts.

Indeed, most of the outstanding thinkers of the latter

part of the nineteenth century and the early part of the twentieth century who attempted to develop an ethical system on purely rational or scientific principles—men such as J. S. Mill, Herbert Spencer, and G. G. Simpson —produced moral codes almost identical with the traditional moral codes of Western Europe, which in turn were based upon ancient Judaeo-Christian ideology. Mill and Spencer were frank to admit that they were merely giving a logical and rational framework to traditional concepts, and that for all practical purposes the traditional morality of Western Europe could well serve as a model for human action.

Quite apart from other considerations, the study of tradition and traditions can be of great value to us in estimating the suitability or unsuitability of any particular social or political institution. The fact that a social or political institution has endured for several generations or even for many centuries does not necessarily mean that it is good and worthy of preservation, and we know that many ancient institutions become hopelessly corrupt and that others cease to perform any useful function. But we must also bear in mind that when a social or political institution has persisted over a long period of time and shows no sign of natural decay, it is apparently well suited to human nature, or at least to the nature of the persons who live under it. In such circumstances it would scarcely be advisable to discard such an institution in favor of a new one which may theoretically be perfect, but whose suitability to a given people has not been tested. Here we still have much to learn from Montesquieu and Burke, both of whom pointed out that a social or political institution to be effective or successful must be in accord with the "spirit" (i.e., the tradition) of the people. Since different peoples still have different traditions, we must look with serious doubts at any attempt to impose uniform institutions upon all the peoples of the earth.[3]

By way of summary we may say that every *science,* including political science to the extent that there is such a science, must be based exclusively upon the logico-empirical method; but because of its inherent limitations this method alone does not and can not give us a complete picture of reality, especially where value judgments are concerned. For this reason all *philosophy,* including political philosophy, must make tentative and cautious use of non-logico-experimental methods such as intuition and tradition in order to secure a more adequate picture of the living world. Nevertheless, we must bear in mind that these other methods are only partially subject to objective verification. Since we cannot be absolutely sure which intuitions are to be accepted and which rejected, or which traditions we may call good and which bad, we cannot expect absolute certainty and complete agreement of thought with respect to any philosophical system or any broad political theory. We can, however, say that a greater knowledge of human nature and of what mankind has accomplished under the sway of different philosophical concepts, should give at least the more thoughtful of us deeper and firmer convictions and a greater degree of unanimity.

[3] We have used the word "tradition" in a general and comprehensive sense. Of course there are many different types and forms of tradition. At times tradition implies the general feeling or beliefs of a people as derived from their immediate forebears. At other times a tradition can be traced back to the actions or sayings of distinguished persons in the more remote past—persons who had or are supposed to have had greater "insight" into reality or into human relations than the bulk of mankind. For present purposes it is not important to distinguish between the different types of tradition.

[4]

The Nature of Man and His World

DETERMINISM AND INDETERMINISM

EVERY POLITICAL PHILOSOPHY of any consequence is based, either consciously or unconsciously, upon certain presuppositions regarding the nature of the world and of man. We need not pause long on the problem of the nature of the external world. Here we can confine ourselves to stating that the scientific developments of the last fifty years have shown conclusively that the universe is far more complex and far more mysterious than was imagined by the leading scientists of the eighteenth and nineteenth centuries. Under the sway of the Newtonian physics most scientists gave a wholehearted mechanical interpretation of the physical world. The world according to this view consisted of nothing but matter and motion, or rather a fixed amount of indestructible and inert matter acted on by certain blind but measurable forces in such a way as to move in a mathematically calculable manner. As matter was inert and as its motion was completely determined by the mechanical forces which acted upon it, it followed that the whole world was completely deterministic in character. It was believed that a scientist with a complete knowledge of mechanics would be able to foretell every development in the universe millenia upon millennia in advance. Finally, it was believed that this matter and motion operated in a framework of an eternal and infinite space and an eternal and infinite time.

Many scientists felt that the theory that nothing exists except matter put in motion by certain natural forces could be applied not only to the physical but also to the biological and psychological worlds. With further knowledge we would see how the same laws which made the planets swing in their orbits could be made to explain how plants and animals were formed and why they behave as they do. Ultimately the likes and dislikes which human beings feel for one another would be seen as nothing more than a special application of the mechanical laws of attraction and repulsion. Even such phenomena as consciousness and thought would be explained by purely mechanical principles. Finally, it was assumed that the principle of rigid determinism, the absence of chance or free will, applied just as much to biological and psychological worlds as to the physical world. This type of thinking had a great influence on many political philosophers. It led them to believe that man was an automaton propelled by a single force—for example, the quest of pleasure, or rational self-interest.

The astounding scientific developments in the first half of the twentieth century greatly transformed our conception of the external world. While the leading scientists are still in sharp disagreement as to the true nature of ultimate reality, most of them concede that the old concepts of a mechanical, deterministic, and materialistic universe have proved crude and naive and must be abandoned. Nearly all of them are now agreed that the universe is not rigidly deterministic, and that with respect to any one physical unit we must speak of probable rather than inevitable developments. Most of them believe that space and time are not two separate things, but different aspects of one ultimate reality, that both are not infinite but finite, and that space itself must be regarded as somehow curved. Similarly, the universe itself must be regarded as finite and yet constantly expanding. The old concept of force has almost been abandoned; in its place the concept of energy has arisen; and it is now known that matter and energy are not two different things, one acting upon the other, but rather two different phases of the same thing. In fact it is now generally believed that matter, energy, space, and time are all derivatives from some more fundamental entity or entities.

The new scientific advances have given a rude jolt to old attempts to explain all biological and psychological factors on a deterministic and mechanical basis. The development of non-determinism has shown the theory that man possesses some kind of free will to be something more than an illusion. While it is still true that all organic bodies must obey certain physical and chemical laws, it is no longer believed that a greater knowledge of physical and chemical laws would explain the development of all organic life, for there are many factors in organic life which cannot be accounted for by any known physical or chemical law. Animals in general and men in particular are now seen to be far more complicated than was once imagined. Any attempt to account for human behavior by a few simple laws or by a list of a few "motivating forces" is bound to lead us into error.

As students of political philosophy it is not our function to make a detailed examination of the many new theories which have evolved in the natural sciences in the last few decades. Even more clearly, it is not our function to judge the respective merits of these various scientific theories where, as is frequently the case, there is marked conflict. But as students of political theory we must bear in mind that, however sharply modern scientists disagree with one another, they are practically in accord in stating that the narrow dogmatism of the earlier scientists was clearly wrong; that the more we investigate the true nature of ultimate reality the more elusive it becomes. Every day it becomes more obvious that "there are many more things in heaven and earth" than were dreamed of in the scientific outlook of half a century ago. We are thus free to re-examine and tentatively accept many theories seemingly outlawed by the science which existed in the time of our grandfathers.

We need not be startled that in place of the previous materialism, several prominent scientists advocate the doctrine that matter and mind are really one and that ultimate reality is as much mental or spiritual as it is material. Of even greater significance is the fact that, in contrast with the atheism so fashionable in scientific circles in the nineteenth century, a large section of the scientific world today finds it not only possible but even necessary to believe in some sort of a Supreme Being, though the impossibility for our finite minds to gain a comprehensive or even an adequate concept of the true nature of this Being is recognized. To find similar beliefs among political philosophers is not surprising. It is probable that the vast majority of the conservative liberals believe in the existence of a Diety; and it is certain that nearly all of them realize that the bulk of mankind will continue to believe in some kind of God and that this fact must be borne in mind when we try to formulate a political theory suitable to the present age.

HEREDITY AND ENVIRONMENT

When we deal with the problem of the nature of man, it is necessary to review not only the ideas of various political philosophers but also recent developments in biology, anthropology, and psychology.

One of the most important problems to be faced is the old question as to the equality or inequality of man. Throughout history nearly all radicals have tended to argue that "all men are created equal," that "naturally" and "essentially" no man is superior or inferior to any other man; that the differences between men are superficial and unimportant, and that what differences do exist are due entirely or at least in large part to differences in environment and upbringing. In like manner, throughout history most, though not all, conservatives have tended to stress the inequality of man, claiming that some are "naturally" and innately superior to others and thus constitute a "natural aristocracy." Many conservatives have added that such superiority or inferiority tends to be an hereditary trait, superior parents tending to produce superior children.

Developments in biology during recent decades have given us certain facts which permit a partial solution of this ancient problem. Biology is far from being an exact science, and the final answer continues to lie in the future, but at least a number of facts appear more or less certain. In the first place, modern biology shows that many of the old arguments were based upon an inexact use of terms. The very terms "equal" and "unequal" are inappropriate, as they imply unprovable value judgments. For one man to be stronger or fleeter than another does not mean that he is thereby "superior"; in other ways he may well be "inferior." That a man is color blind does not mean that morally or intellectually he is inferior to those who do not suffer from color blindness. A man may have very "superior" capabilities in mathematics or music and yet be very inferior in other respects. One man may demonstrate far greater "qualities of leadership" than other men, but these qualities may make him either a national hero or a criminal chief.

In place of the old arguments about equality and inequality it would be far better to pose the problem of differentiation and non-differentiation. Are all men more or less the same, or do they differ in their physical, moral, and intellectual character? To this question there is only one possible answer: Men do differ, and differ profoundly, in many essential ways. To ignore these differences is not only ridiculous but dangerous. Everywhere we look we see big men and little men, strong men and weak men, saints and criminals, aggressive men and submissive men, talented men and untalented men, wise men and fools. These differences may be manifested in different ways. One man may be strong and foolish, another strong and wise. One may be an intellectual genius and a criminal, another may be an intellectual giant and a saint. Even within the intellectual field there are vast differences. A man may be a genius in mathematics or nuclear physics, and yet be incapable of absorbing the data provided by the biological or the social sciences.

But even if this differentiation of mankind be admitted, the problem remains: are these differences innate or acquired—are they due to heredity or to environment? The vast majority of biologists would answer that some differences are primarily innate and hereditary and others primarily acquired as the result of environment, but that in most cases differences are due partly to heredity and partly to environment. It is sometimes possible to give approximate figures as to the relative importance of the two factors. In some cases it seems probable that heredity accounts for 75 per cent of the result and environment for only 25 per cent. In other cases these proportions are exactly reversed. In many cases, however, it is impossible to given even approximate percentages, and the most that can be said is that heredity and environment as governing facts appear to be more or less equal.

At any rate, it is clear that Locke was quite wrong in implying that all children are born exactly alike and that all subsequent differences are due merely to variations in upbringing. It is now beyond question that children are born with many different characteristics, and that most of these differences are due to differences in hereditary background. Some are born color blind, other are not; some are born tone deaf, others are not. Because of hereditary factors, to about 70 per cent of all Americans, a chemical substance known as P.T.C. (or phenyl-thio-carbamide) has an intensely bitter taste; to the other 30 per cent it is completely tasteless. It is known that certain diseases are due largely or entirely to hereditary causes. Thus some are born to suffer from haemophilia, and others are not. Whether a man does not develop diabetes depends in large measure upon his heredity. The same is true of some (but not all) allergies, and of certain (though not all) types of idiocy and insanity. It is also known that many emotional and intellectual characteristics may not be evident at birth and only become important in later years. A study of identical twins separated at birth (and thus with different environments) shows that they tend to resemble each other not only physically but also emotionally and mentally. They tend to make similar records in school. Where one such twin shows criminal tendencies, there is a strong likelihood that similar tendencies will develop in the other twin.

The fact that certain differences between men are due to differences in heredity is a fact of major importance, and one not to be neglected in political science. At the same time we must be careful not to give undue weight to heredity. Many of the differences and defects caused by heredity can be compensated for by changes in the environment. Many children are born with defective vision, but in most cases this defective vision can be corrected by the use of glasses. Although heredity predisposes a man to diabetes, nearly all diabetics can now lead normal lives if they are treated with insulin. Because of his heredity a boy may have a tendency to grow tall, but his growth may be stunted by the absence of proper food. Mental ability, though strongly influenced by heredity, can be enormously modified by environmental factors.

Above all, it is essential that we distinguish between genuine facts regarding hereditary differences on the one hand and numerous fantastic theories regarding race on the other. In many cases heredity can and does explain how one individual differs from another. To a limited extent we can apply the rules of heredity to show how certain characteristics sometimes persist in families for several generations. But we must remember that parents transmit different genes and chromosomes (the building blocks of heredity) to each one of their children, so that, apart from identical twins, even full brothers and sisters may differ radically from one another with respect to the physical, emotional, and intellectual characteristics they have inherited. We frequently find, for instance, an unusually bright man with an unusually stupid brother.

When we examine larger groups, such as the so-called "races," it is usually impossible to assign any characteristics which are common to all members. We must remember that the transmission of physical and non-physical characteristics very seldom go hand in hand. A blue-eyed man with a marked mathematical ability and a brown-eyed woman with little or no mathematical ability may produce a child with the brown eyes of the mother and the mathematical ability of the father, or they may produce a child with the blue eyes of the father and the absence of mathematical ability of the mother. Since one characteristic is not necessarily tied to another, we cannot tell whether a man is courageous or cowardly, musical or unmusical, intelligent or stupid from the color of his eyes, his stature, or the shape of his head.

GEOGRAPHY AND ECONOMY

If the ultra-radicals were wrong in making environment account for everything, the ultra-conservatives were equally wrong in making heredity account for everything, for environment in various forms plays a major, sometimes *the* major role in the development of human affairs, both individually and collectively. Montesquieu was naive and crude—sometimes altogether erroneous in some of his theories—but he was undoubtedly right in claiming that climate and other geographic factors exert a strong influence upon human society. In the last few years Ellsworth Huntington and other scientific geographers have shown that many phases of human history can be understood only in the light of the climate and climatic changes in specific areas. It is more than a coincidence that in ancient times civilization started in hot treeless plains, such as the Nile valley and the "Fertile Crescent" of the Near East, and only spread much later to the colder, forested areas of the north. It is a fact that many of the migrations of peoples which profoundly influenced later history were associated with marked changes in the rainfall of certain areas, which affected the land's fertility. It is certain that the establishment and persistence of Negro slavery in the southern portion of the United States and its rejection in the northern portion was due in large measure to climatic differences in the two areas.

In addition to climate, many other geographic factors affect human society. Not infrequently the physical configuration of an area has a significant effect upon the life of its inhabitants. Open plains invite settlement and facilitate communications and the migrations of peoples. Mountainous regions make communications and migrations more difficult. Not infrequently such regions are inhabited by refugees who have been defeated and driven out of their ancestral homes on the plains. The distribution of waterways often strongly influences social and economic developments. Large communities are apt to grow at or near the mouth of large rivers (e.g., New Orleans) or near the confluence of two major tributaries (e.g., St. Louis) or at the juncture between two waterway systems (e.g., Chicago). We can often observe how the soil of a country determines whether the inhabitants devote themselves primarily to sheep raising, to agriculture, or to commerce. Time after time history has been altered by the invasion and conquest of rich agricultural areas by rough nomads from arid pasture lands. In modern times the presence or absence of certain basic minerals in a territory has been of immense influence upon the economic and political life of a nation. Industrial development usually begins where such raw materials as iron ore and coal are found in abundance and in close proximity. Later still, the exhaustion of such minerals and the need for still further raw materials have led to numerous wars of conquest. Indeed, the theory of the "pull of the heavy commodity" further bears this out. Economic historians hold that in industrial development, requiring a number of essential raw materials, the location of the industry will invariably tend to be pulled toward or to the source of the heaviest commodity—usually of course one of the raw materials, but at times such a commodity as the food for the workers. Japan's expansion into North China and movement of industry to the mainland of Asia nearer coal and ore is a case in point.

Closely connected with the geographic factors are those which may be called economic. Whether a nation is primarily pastoral, or agricultural, or industrial is bound to have profound political repercussions. In a country inhabited partly by shepherds, partly by agrarians, and partly by artisans and merchants there is commonly a sharp political struggle for control. When a primarily agrarian country changes to a primarily industrial one there is usually a marked shift in the balance of political power. As Aristotle pointed out over two thousand years ago, when a country is rigidly divided between a few very rich and a many very poor there are apt to be political convulsions. As Aristotle also made evident, comparative political stability is usually achieved only when there is a large and powerful middle class able to mediate between the rich and the poor. Many centuries later Harrington was able to establish the rule that there is a tendency for political power to rise out of economic power and that it is difficult for a small oligarchy to remain in control of a state in which there is a wide distribution of wealth. In modern times Marx and his followers were able to picture, though highly exaggerate, the intimate relation which sometimes exists between economic and political organizations.

We must, however, avoid extremes. Just as we have learned that heredity is an important, but not the only factor influencing human behavior, so must we be careful to bear in mind that environment is not the only factor. Moreover, we must never forget that there are many different types of environmental factors, and that no one of them is all-important; neither environment as a whole nor any one of the various environmental factors is a *determinant* or cause of human behavior. Environmental factors can at best only *condition* or influence human behavior to a greater or lesser extent at different times and places. Sometimes climate and terrain play an extremely significant role in the development of human institutions. Sometimes they are relatively unimportant. And sometimes humanity develops in a way directly contrary to what a knowledge of the various geographic conditions would lead one to expect: The Egyptian and Mesopotamian civilizations started in hot treeless plains, but the Mayan civilization, the highest of the Pre-Columbian American cultures, developed in a tropical jungle. Appreciable deposits of coal and iron tend to facilitate the industrialization of an area, but they had no effect on North America until the coming of Europeans.

Similarly the effect of economic factors upon human behavior must not be exaggerated. Aristotle, Harrington, and Marx were undoubtedly right in claiming that economic conditions in many cases have exerted an important influence upon social and political institutions. But Marx, the most extreme of the three, was undoubtedly mistaken in insisting that the economic factor was not only the most important but the sole determinant. While it is true that in many cases economics has influenced political developments, it is also true that in many other cases politics has strongly influenced economic developments. Contrary to the theory of economic determinism, the most fanatical devotees of communism have come not from the starving proletariat but rather from comfortably situated middle-class intellectuals. In

Italy, to take only one example, the northern section is far more prosperous than the southern section, but it is in the north rather than in the south that Communism has won the greatest number of converts. Following his belief in economic determinism, Marx dogmatically asserted that Communism would and could arise only in areas which had developed a high degree of capitalistic industrialization, such as England, Germany, France, and the United States. In reality the Communists have come to power in such primarily agrarian countries as Russia and China, in which capitalism and industrialization were in very low stages of development.

In the nineteenth century and in the early years of the twentieth century, the Marxian theory of economic determinism won a large following among persons who did not accept the other dogmas of Communism. More careful study has shown the theory is fundamentally erroneous. As Crane Brinton remarks, "We are now well out of the once fashionable and innocent economic materialism that explained all human group conflicts as a struggle for economic goods."[1] Even the socialists who once tended to accept this dogma now reject it. Thus we find R. H. S. Crossman, the editor of the *New Fabian Essays,* stating: "It is important . . . not to fall into the materialist fallacy of assuming that economics is the prime motive of human action . . . the belief that economics are the determinant factor in social change [is] a vicious fallacy."[2] Norman Thomas, leader of the American Socialists, comes to the same conclusion: "In the light of modern psychology, our own observation of human conduct, and our fuller knowledge of ancient cultures, it is certainly untenable to hold the rigid view of the materialistic conception of history which Marx

[1] Brinton, *The Shaping of the Modern Mind,* p. 16.
[2] *New Fabian Essays,* pp. 11, 21.

advanced, a conception which declares that the prevailing economic system determines the general character of the political and intellectual life of the epoch."[3]

REASON AND PSYCHE

We have seen how in some cases heredity and in others environment plays a direct and predominant part in conditioning human behavior. But it should also be borne in mind that on many occasions the most important factors are those we may call "psychic" or psychological —special faculties or phenomena of the human mind. Ultimately these psychic factors can be traced back to the action and interaction of heredity and environment, but because of their special character and their unique importance it is well to give them separate consideration. These psychic factors fall into two main groups: one consisting primarily of the faculty of reason, and the other of various non-rational emotions and instincts. Both groups are present, or at least latent, in all normal infants (and hence are "innate" or at least controlled by the laws of heredity) ; both reason and the emotions come into operation slowly and gradually, as the infant matures physically, and during this period these psychic faculties are subject to strong and effective environmental influence.

In former times, especially during the eighteenth century, the scope and power of reason was greatly exaggerated. It is now known that its scope is limited and that there are certain problems with which it does not and can not effectively deal. Ordinary human behavior is far less controlled by reason than was once claimed by some of the philosophers. It is simply not true that man's social and political actions are based primarily

[3] *Democratic Socialism,* p. 9.

upon reason or that man normally does what reason tells him to do. It is not even true, as Bentham claimed, that man is motivated primarily by rational self-interest and that because of this rational self-interest men always buy in the cheapest and sell in the dearest market. Experience proves that men frequently perform actions which any reasoning would show not to be in their self-interest.

Yet it would be absurd to lapse into complete irrationalism and deny or underrate the value and importance of reason. "Man is a rational animal," to use Aristotle's phrase, not in the sense that man is dominated by reason, but in the sense that man is the only animal capable of making use of conscious reason; and because of this very fact, man is able to master all other animals. It is reason, (combined with observation and experiment) which has permitted man to build the majestic edifice of modern science; and it is this science based upon reason which has enabled man to create a highly developed technology and rendered him capable of transforming the whole face of the planet. Reason alone does not and can not give us an adequate set of values, but once these values have been acquired by other means, it is reason which enables men to implement them effectively—to accomplish the things which men come to believe are worth accomplishing.

But important as reason is, it is certain that men are normally much more influenced by the basic emotions and instincts, those psychic factors which are non-rational in character. Some psychologists attempt to deny the very existence of such factors, but the vast majority not only assert their existence but stress the important role that they play in human life. Philosophers have not infrequently tried to explain human motivation in terms of only one or two simple instincts. Thus Bentham claimed that man is motivated solely by an instinctive desire to gain pleasure and avoid pain. Schopenhauer thought that the primary instinct was the will to live. Nietzsche claimed that it was the will to power. We now realize that this attempt at simplification was erroneous, for man is far from being a simple animal, and at the roots of his being are not one or two but many different emotions and instincts. Unfortunately, psychologists are still in wide disagreement as to which and how many of these emotions and instincts are to be considered basic or primary. Nevertheless, the political philosopher, without attempting to mediate in this disagreement, can choose from this mass of emotions and instincts—whether primary or secondary, whether simple or complex—those which have proved of major significance in the development of social and political institutions and tell how each such factor tends to influence human behavior.

A notable factor to be taken into consideration is sex, or as Lester Ward preferred to call it, the instinct of reproduction. Sex is certainly no recent discovery; man did not have to wait until modern times to learn of the important role it plays directly in social and indirectly in political life. Nevertheless, during the latter part of the nineteenth and the early part of the twentieth centuries there was a tremendous increase in the study of the sexual impulse, owing largely to the work of Freud and other psychoanalysts. It is undoubtedly true that Freud's work is and will continue to be of interest and value to the scientific world in showing the wide ramifications of the sexual impulse and how certain sexual desires can be repressed in the conscious mind and yet linger in the unconscious mind. Yet it is also true that Freud and the orthodox Freudians have greatly over-emphasized the role which sex plays in human life. They are as onesided when they attempt to explain the whole of history in terms of sex as are the Marxists when they attempt to explain everything in terms of economics.

Two other psychic factors important in the development of human institutions are the desire for innovation or change on the one hand and the desire for stability or permanence on the other. The one factor leads to the creation and acceptance of new ideas or theories (some good, some bad) ; to the creation of new musical and artistic forms; new fashions in clothes; to the attempt to construct new social and economic systems. The other, a counterbalancing factor, leads a man to accept existing mores, traditional ideas, and value judgments; to preserve previously established social, economic, and political institutions.

It is obvious that both of these two psychic factors, in direct conflict with each other, are possessed by every normal human being to a greater or a lesser extent. Every great innovator is a traditionalist on some point, and every great traditionalist at some point or other shows a passionate desire for innovation. Jefferson was a great innovator, who protested vigorously that the present should not be ruled by the dead hand of the past; but, for all of his love of innovation, he willingly accepted the century-old political philosophy of Locke, stoutly defended the traditional Christian moral code, and was almost lyrical in his praise of the Graeco-Roman standards of art and architecture. St. Thomas Aquinas is usually regarded as a great exponent of traditionalism, and certainly he had a profound reverence for the ideas which came down from the past; but he was a great innovator when he made a startling new attempt to reconcile and synthesize the philosophical ideas of Plato and Aristotle with the religious dogmas of the great church fathers.

Although all men have both the instinct of innovation and the instinct of stability, with some men and with some groups at various times and places one instinct is more developed and more powerful than the other. Dispassionate examination of the matter indicates that man individually and human society as a whole have need of both instincts and should attempt to develop them more or less equally.

Change or innovation of some sort is not only inevitable, but also essential to human well-being. Immobility or rigidity means death. New ideas, new ways of looking at things, new literary and artistic forms, and modification of existing social and political institutions are necessary to prevent stagnation and decay. Certainly most great material and intellectual advances have been made when a large portion of a population has been interested in new inventions and been willing to formulate and accept new ideas. But all change is not necessarily progress and all innovation is not necessarily reform. Not infrequently a large segment of the population is led into serious error by blindly following some new fad or accepting some new cult simply because it is new. When the instinct for innovation is overdeveloped or overemphasized, the whole structure of society tends to be undermined.

The instinct for stability can also lead to both unfortunate and fortunate consequences. At times it has led to the fanatical defense of discredited ideas and outmoded institutions; and at times it has prompted society to persecute and even to kill men making or seeking to make significant contributions to scientific or philo-

sophic thought. But on many other occasions the instinct
for stability has led men to preserve ideas and institutions which have proved useful and valuable. It has
helped to preserve the accumulated wisdom of our ancestors and respect for family life, the foundation stone
of healthy social life. It has set before us for our admiration and imitation the figures of the wise, the just,
and the good of the past.

Modern psychology and sociology have shown the
enormously important role which tradition plays in the
development of human beings even when they are not
aware of it: "The individual, bare, naked and unqualified by social pressures and social tradition is a thing
unknown to history or experience; that which we call
the individual is always and everywhere a being molded
by those around him and those who have gone before
him, a being who may please to think himself independent of his fellows, but who in reality is little more than
a puppet in their hands, a being whose conception of
the world he sees around him, whose moral and social
standards, whose belief about nature and the unseen
powers about nature, whose very reason, will and conscience are determined almost entirely by the beliefs,
customs and traditions into which, with no choice of
his own, he happens to be born."[4]

Tradition has also played and still plays a major part
in civilizing mankind and in restraining his more bar-
baric and animal instincts and emotions. We do not have
to believe with Calvin that man is totally depraved; but
contrary to the naive optimism of the nineteenth century,
we now realize that there is still a great deal of "original
sin" in man—or, to say the same thing non-theologically,

[4] Vaughan, *Studies in the History of Political Philosophy,* vol. 2,
p. 39.

that man has many instincts in common with the wolf and the tiger. From early times the old, wild animal side of human nature has been checked primarily by the iron yoke of customary law. When tradition has been shattered, and all respect for it gone, the secret and long-suppressed animal instincts are likely to spring out again, and we witness scenes of cruelty and horror, as happened during the French Revolution, and more recently in Nazi Germany and in Communist Russia.

The last few decades have brought to light another condition likely to arise when traditional values and institutions have been destroyed. During the last hundred and fifty years, the influx of Europeans into all parts of Africa and Asia has resulted in some curious developments. In some parts of Africa the Negroes have managed in large measure to maintain their native beliefs and customs and their tribal organization; but in many other areas the Negroes have been completely "detribalized," and their ancient mode of life and their ancient beliefs and customs have disappeared. In Asia a similar development has taken place: some Asiatics have remained true to the manners, customs, family life, and religious doctrines of their ancestors, but many others have become "deracinated" or uprooted, abandoning their ancient ways of life and their traditional social institutions and standards of value. Many such persons have willingly taken over the best modern European technical devices, but only rarely have they adopted European moral and spiritual ideals.

Both in Africa and in Asia the abandonment of traditional values and traditional institutions has usually been unfortunate. The "detribalized" Negroes of Africa and the "deracinated" peoples of Asia have usually been restless, uneasy, and unhappy. Consciously or unconsciously, they have been groping for some guide, some support, some new standard for action and belief; and for this reason they are the section of the population most subject to Communist infiltration. The Communist set of dogmas, in spite of its many absurdities, provides a sort of "spiritual security" for those whose ancient set of beliefs and values have been destroyed. Contrary to Marxist theory, the turning of a particular people or a particular section of a people to Communism usually has nothing to do with economic status or standard of living; it is much more often a question of whether or not they have been deprived of or have voluntarily abandoned their traditional modes of belief and behavior.

In Nigeria, for example, the Hausa of the north are just as poor if not poorer than the Ilos and Yorubas of the south, but the Hausa have kept their traditional ideas, customs, and institutions and hence are scarcely touched by Communist propaganda. The Ilos and Yorubas, on the other hand, in spite of their economic progress, have been largely detribalized, and as a consequence have been very susceptible to the blandishments of Soviet agents. In Kenya the bloody Mao Mao movement is as yet confined to the Kikuyu, the most "detribalized" of all the Negro peoples in this area. Similarly in Asia: in China the rapid decay of the old Confucian codes and standards during the last fifty years paved the way for the Communist sweep of the country. Chinese Communism owes its rise, not to the oppressed and exploited factory workers of the great cities, but to a devoted group of "deracinated" intellectuals, nearly all of them of middle class origin. If India goes Communist it will not be because of the spontaneous uprising of the masses, who though desperately poor are still mostly orthodox Hindus; it will be due to the small "emancipated" student and professional groups who have deliberately turned their backs on their Hindu heritage.

INDIVIDUALISM AND GREGARIOUSNESS

Two further basic emotions or instincts of great importance in motivating human behavior are the tendency towards individualism or self-assertion and the tendency towards sociability or gregariousness, which implies the voluntary submission of the individual to group control. It is obvious that these two instincts are in direct contrast with each other, but that all normal men possess both to a greater or lesser degree—at certain times and places being primarily influenced by the instinct towards individual assertion and at others primarily by the tendency towards gregariousness.

The instinct towards individualism is rooted in the basic desire for self-preservation. In order to survive, practically all men think it necessary to look after their own interest to some extent—sometimes to a very great extent. Bentham thought that all men are motivated solely by rational self-interest; but modern psychology has shown us that self-interest is not always rational, and that self-interest of any sort is not the sole motivating force in human behavior. There is no denying, however, that self-interest is a very important factor in conditioning the actions of practically all human beings. Sometimes this instinct is concerned only with survival; but in most cases the instinct for self-assertion makes a man seek the respect, admiration, or even affection and love of other persons. Not infrequently this same instinct makes a man want to influence or dominate others, for in most cases men have not only a will to live but also a will to power.

Man's instinct of self-assertion is present at all times

and at all places. Even in very early times, when men lived in small, compact, tightly knit kinship groups, there was competition between different members of the group, as each man sought the reputation of being braver, or wiser, or more able than his fellows. But there can be no doubt that, broadly speaking the instinct of self-assertion has been given freer rein in modern times. Rome's legal recognition, for the first time, of the individual *qua* individual and the subsequent development of the Christian doctrine of individual responsibility led to the theory of the dignity and worth of the individual which has played an important part in the shaping of modern Western culture.

Since the instinct of self-assertion, as long as it is kept within limits, plays a useful and necessary part in the proper development of mankind, competition of some sort must be kept as an integral part of social, economic, and political life. The competition may be for a laurel leaf, the medal of an order, or a sack of gold (although in most cases it is necessary that a man be offered a choice or a mixture of all three if he is to be incited to appropriate action). Without competition a society becomes hopelessly stagnant—as most of the present-day Fabian Socialists are now frank to admit. Worse still, if society is unwilling or unable to give a larger reward for superior action, it finds itself forced to mete out severe punishment for inferior action in order to try to mantain social and political progress.

But if the instinct of self-assertion plays a very valuable role in human life if kept within bounds, it can also prove injurious and even disastrous if permitted to overstep these bounds. It is not true, as Bentham asserted, that every man working for his own self-interest automatically works for the ultimate benefit of society. To be sure, many actions motivated by self-interest redound ultimately to the benefit of society; but in many other cases such actions are seriously harmful to society and if practiced on a large enough scale will lead to its destruction. The vast majority of acts which we call crimes and punish as such are nothing more than acts which are motivated by self-interest, but which injure the other members of society. Murder, robbery, and arson, in nearly all cases are motivated by self-interest, but they are rightly punished by society as injuries to itself. And even though there be no question of crime, whenever large sections of society, whether capitalists or members of the proletariat, are concerned exclusively with promoting their own interests irrespective of the interest of other groups, the society is in imminent danger of disintegration.

It is thus fortunate that man is provided with the basic instinct of gregariousness or sociability to check his instinct of self-assertion. It is not true that men are essentially benevolent or altruistic; but it is true that nearly all men delight in being a member of some group for which they are willing to make great self-sacrifice in order to maintain their membership—i.e., to continue to be accepted as in "good standing" by the other members of the group. Man is a group-forming animal, and much of his behavior can be understood only in the light of this fact. Modern research has shown that the old theory that man originally lived in "a state of nature" characterized by the atomic isolation of each individual is complete nonsense. Archaeology and anthropology have demonstrated that long before the beginnings of recorded history men were living in close and intimate union as members of small groups which exercised enormous control over them.

All of these early groups were kinship groups—all the members being, in theory at least, descended from a common (sometimes mythical) ancestor. In later times, with the conquest of one group by another and the formation of new social and political units, the old compact kinship groups tended to disintegrate and disappear. But the group-forming instinct of mankind was so strong that new groups formed to take their place. Sometimes these groups took the form of castes or of "big families" as in China, or of "small families" as in Europe since the time of Christ. But even these were not enough to satisfy man's basic social instinct. Under changing conditions new groups arose and still continue to arise. Some of these groups are occupational, as are "guilds" or labor unions or chambers of commerce. Some are semi-occupational, like the recently established service clubs (e.g., Rotary). Others have a religious basis. Others are purely social, as in the case of fraternities and sororities and their adult counterparts. All such groups have long played and still play an important role in human life; but since about 1500 A.D. most of them have been more and more subordinated to the group known as the nation-state. It is possible that eventually the various nation-states may be included in a still wider unit, but because of the strong emotional appeal which nationalism evokes, such a development cannot now be foreseen.

Man's forming of groups has had both favorable and unfavorable consequences. Most of the actions which we customarily call altruistic or benevolent are inspired by the voluntary subordination of the individual to one or another of the groups to which he belongs. A man, or more frequently a woman, will sacrifice himself or herself for the benefit of the family. Men on many occasions have braved torture and death in defense of their religious organizations. Millions have been killed so that the nation to which they belong might preserve its integrity and independence. Groups, moreover, have generally been effective in maintaining some kind of moral discipline among their members. Almost all groups have a rather clearly formulated code of ethics, by which most men are willing to abide rather than risk expulsion. Standards of moral behavior are thus established not only by religious organizations but also by professional associations, and even service clubs. It is not going too far to say that the group in socializing man has also moralized him.

But group activity has also had many unfavorable consequences. Here we must distinguish between organized and integrated groups on the one hand and unorganized and non-integrated groups on the other. The non-integrated group is a crowd, a mob, a mass; its activity is nearly always harmful to the community. The crowd or the mob is usually guided by temporary but passionate mass hysteria, leading to riots and other forms of collective violence. The integrated group has a more permanent character and is controlled by a certain discipline. It is usually organized on a hierarchic or semi-hierarchic basis, and the members of the hierarchy are forced to shoulder some responsibility for the actions of the group. The integrated group is far superior to the non-integrated group, and its actions are apt to be far more beneficial; but even the actions of the integrated group can on occasion prove to be extremely harmful. Thus the members of one group in an excess of group solidarity may cause severe damage to members of other groups in the same community. The actions of two conflicting religious groups within a single nation may lead to civil war. Too vigorous action on the part of an association of manufacturers may result in the exploitation of the working people. In like manner too vigorous action on the part of labor unions may deal a death blow to the economy of an entire country. More important, the actions of any and all groups, if permitted to go unchecked, are almost certain to lead to the suppression of all individual expression and activity, an end not to be desired.

In sum, if individualism is unchecked by some mode of group control, the result is anarchy; but if group activity is unchecked by some form of individualism, the result is tyranny. Groups play a very useful role when they punish acts which are clearly antisocial, but they do irreparable harm when they cause the well of individual initiative to dry up. It is primarily to the individual that we must look for action; the proper role of the group is to prevent individual action from becoming antisocial in character.

RATIONALIZATION AND MYTH

Another basic emotion or instinct which plays an important part in forming social and political institutions is the tendency, common to nearly all men, to give a pseudo-rational veneer to their own wishes and desires. Close analysis shows that many of the ideas and ideologies current among men are the results of wishful thinking rather than abstract reason. Men reach a position because of their emotions and then attempt to persuade others (and often themselves) that this position has been reached by logical induction or deduction. The program of a political party, actually planned to appeal to the selfish desires of certain powerful groups, is in nearly all cases phrased to appear as sound argument for measures of benefit to the country as a whole.

This basic emotion or instinct may be called the "myth-making" faculty, for it results in the production of mental images which most European scientists have agreed to call "myths." A myth may be defined as a body of mental images or ideas capable of evoking strong emotions leading to action. The mental image, the idea, the "myth," may be true and based on sound reasoning; or it may be completely absurd, based upon an absolute misstatement or misrepresentation of facts. In any case, the "myth" is important, because it is capable of widespread acceptance, and because, once accepted, it supplies an emotional drive that gives cohesion to a group and enables it to undertake positive action. Every important social and political movement in history has been in a large measure the result of widespread acceptance of some myth. The eighteenth century idea of a prepolitical state of nature and the belief that all states originate in a social contract were "myths" bearing little semblance to reality, but these doctrines radically transformed the course of history. The Marxian dogmas of dialectic materialism and of surplus value are accepted by no impartial scientist, but as "myths" they have been extremely effective in aiding the spread of Communism.

RADICAL AND CONSERVATIVE VIEWS OF MAN

After surveying the main characteristics of human nature, we can give a tentative answer to some of the problems which political philosophers have debated for centuries. For example, most radical philosophers have based their political systems upon the idea that men are equal, rational, and good, while most conservatives have insisted that men are unequal, irrational, and more nearly bad than good. If our survey of human nature be correct, we can now say that both radicals and conservatives were partially right and partially wrong, although it seems to us that the conservatives were probably a little closer to the truth than the radicals.

The radicals were right in insisting that a man's "superiority" or "inferiority" does not necessarily depend upon his economic background or the social status of his ancestors. They were right in insisting that a man's intellectual capacity does not depend upon the color of his skin or the texture of his hair. They were right in insisting that many seeming inequalities are artificial in character and not based upon "natural" inequalities. But the conservatives were right in insisting that all men are *not* alike, that they differ radically from one another in temperament, in their reaction to external stimuli, and in their intellectual capabilities. We have seen that some of these differences are due to variations in biological heritage, and that some, between various ethnic and national groups, are due primarily to environmental divergences in traditional and cultural backgrounds. We have also seen that such differences, whatever their origin, are much harder to eliminate or overcome than was once imagined; and we must conclude that until such differences have been eliminated or transformed it would be disastrous to attempt to impose the same social and political institutions upon all the peoples of the world.

The radicals were right in insisting that man is a rational animal, capable of using and benefiting from his rational faculties. But the conservatives were also right in insisting that normally man is much more dominated by his emotions than by his intellect; that in many cases when a man claims to be using his reason he is really guilty of wishful thinking; and that often he is more influenced by "myths" than by facts. Thus, when we consider the realm of politics, we must realize that public opinion is frequently formed by an appeal to nonrational inferences and emotional suggestions; that in many cases men are more susceptible to high sounding names, slogans, symbols, and party shibboleths than to rational arguments.

On the question of the "goodness" or "badness" of man, the radicals—at least those of the school of Locke and Jefferson—were right in claiming that man is not wholly bad, that he is not entirely a depraved animal capable of correction only by force. They were also right in claiming that man is not solely and exclusively motivated by rational or irrational self-interest. All men have a sense of "duty" and obligation urging them to do certain things, even though such a course of action entails a certain amount of self-sacrifice; and although with some men this sense of duty is rather weak, with others it is fairly strong and plays an important role in motivating their actions. Bentham was certainly wrong when he claimed that man is always and inevitably motivated by a desire for personal pleasure.

On the other hand, the conservatives were undoubtedly right when they insisted that there is a great deal of imperfection and evil in human nature, and that any political philosophy which forgets this fact is guilty of a serious error. Man is not entirely corrupt and depraved, but to state that he is, is to come closer to the truth than to state that he is essentially good. In the language of psychology, man is naturally a creature in which purely egoistic tendencies are much stronger than altruistic tendencies. In the language of theology, man is naturally a "sinner," who in the vast majority of cases is apt to "leave undone those things which he ought to have done, and to do those things which he ought not to have done." It is not true that every man in seeking his own happiness automatically enhances the happiness of other persons. While in some cases a man may seek his own happiness without adversely affecting the happiness of others, in most cases the happiness of the com-

munity can only be secured when the egoistic impulses
of the individual are curbed and disciplined by a code—
a moral code, if you will—imposed on him by his family, or by the social, political, and religious organizations to which he happens to belong. Without these
curbs not only is man self-seeking, but in most cases he
seeks to impose his will upon others. Acton was profoundly right in his dictum, "power corrupts, and absolute power corrupts absolutely."

Closely connected with the question of the goodness
and badness of mankind is the question whether or not
it is possible to change human nature. Most of the radicals have argued not only that man is fundamentally
good, but that with a little effort he can be made more
or less perfect. A great many radicals have claimed that
any imperfections shown by humanity are due to bad
environment, ignorance or poverty, and that once these
handicaps have been removed by governmental action,
the innate goodness of man will be completely and immediately realized. The conservatives have usually
claimed not only that man is naturally and fundamentally sinful, but also that it is almost if not absolutely
impossible to change human nature—at least by governmental means.

Again, careful consideration shows that the truth lies
somewhere between these two extremes. However much
we disagree with Herbert Spencer on other matters, we
must admit that he showed sound judgment in his assertion that "human nature is indefinitely modifiable, but
that no modification of it can be brought about rapidly."
The radicals were right in claiming that with sufficient
pressure over a long time it is possible to modify at least
the outward expressions of human character, and ultimately to modify even this character itself. It is true that
universal compulsory education will wipe out illiteracy

and increase the amount of general knowledge available to the average citizen. It is true that compulsory health and sanitation laws can decrease certain types of disease and thus indirectly aid the well-being of the general population. It is true that an overall rise in the standard of living usually, though not invariably, leads to a decrease in certain types of petty crimes.

But the experience of the past few decades has shown that the radicals were hopelessly visionary in thinking human nature can be quickly and drastically changed by simple acts of legislation or by governmental interference. This is true whether the legislator aims at direct modification of human nature or follows T. H. Green and seeks "to remove the handicaps" which prevent man's "better nature" from coming to fruition. The attempts of the Puritans both in England and in America to make men "moral" by means of legal sanctions ended in dismal failure. We can sympathize with Green's efforts to make men sober by removing the "handicap" of the liquor traffic, but we know that "the noble experiment" of prohibition resulted largely in the increase of corruption and organized crime. We have learned that compulsory education can make men able to read, but it does not necessarily make men wise or more rational in their political judgments. We have learned that sometimes efforts by the government to raise the standard of living—price controls, for example—lead chiefly to corruption and black marketeering. We have further learned that even when a rise in economic standards does take place (with or without governmental action), it does not necessarily mean that there is a cessation or even a marked diminution of crime or juvenile delinquency.

In a word, we may say that a well-organized and well-administered government does tend to have a beneficial effect upon both public and private morality, but it is patently inane to imagine that reform of the government or of the laws will or can make a startling transformation in human nature. Those persons who aim to bring about immediate human perfection by changes in the law are guilty of dangerous absurdity. Those who seek by legislative means to create a heaven on earth frequently create conditions which make human life a living hell.

We must also discard as an outworn superstition the notion that human nature automatically improves from generation to generation and that moral progress is constant and inevitable. Sometimes for a century or two we do witness an improvement in standards of morality and in adherence to these standards, but at other periods in history we witness a marked decay of manners and of morals. Unfortunately, it seems that most often improvement in human character and actions takes place slowly and gradually, but that when degeneration sets in it takes place rapidly. There is undoubtedly a reason for this. Man improves only when he submits more and more perfectly to moral codes formulated by the social groups to which he slowly and gradually adjusts himself. When there is a collapse of traditional codes and standards—which frequently takes place at times of great social and political change—the old egoistic instincts in man which have been kept in check are apt to reassert themselves with startling rapidity.

[5]

Ethical Foundations

EUDAEMONIA

WHAT STANDARD OF VALUE we should adopt in judging the goodness and badness of social and political actions is a problem about which philosophers have puzzled and disagreed for over two thousand years. As we have already seen, most scientists agree that the strictly scientific or logico-empirical method, taken by itself, does not and can not give us a standard of value. This method does give the political philosopher an increasingly adequate picture of how states function and how their citizens behave, but it is not able to tell him how states ought to function and how their citizens ought to behave. Yet some standard of value is an absolute necessity for human existence. Almost without exception, man feels that there *is* a good and a bad—even though he may disagree violently with his neighbor as to *what* is good and bad. Even such rigid logico-empiricists as Bertrand Russell, who adamantly deny the existence of a scientific standard of value, are most vociferous in demanding that man be taught or forced to behave in a certain way, and that states be compelled to follow a certain course of action.

For many centuries there have been some philosophers who have claimed that the only valid standard of value is pleasure or happiness—in modern times the most noted exponent of this philosophy being Jeremy Bentham, who attempted to make hedonism into a scientific system. To Bentham each man does and should seek only his own happiness, while the state should seek the greatest happiness of the greatest number. Bentham attracted thousands of followers, and for a while it looked as though his system would be everywhere triumphant. Subsequent generations, however, have found his system of scientific hedonism far from satisfactory. They discovered that Bentham was wrong when he claimed that every man always seeks only his personal happiness. They discovered, moreover, that Bentham's teachings frequently led to unfortunate results: when a man seeks only his happiness he usually finds unhappiness; a man generally finds happiness only when he forgets about the pursuit of happiness and seeks after some other and higher goal. They also discovered that it is almost impossible to maintain a state which aims at the general happiness when that state consists of men motivated primarily by pursuit of their own private pleasures.

Other attempts to establish a purely naturalistic standard of value have also proved hopelessly inadequate, as even the radicals are beginning to realize. During the nineteenth century most radicals were content with a purely hedonistic or materialistic standard. But in the middle of the twentieth century we find such radicals as Norman Thomas asserting: "any and every attempt at an amoral politico-economic system—that is, a system which is independent of ethics, has been fraught with disaster. Pragmatic reformism of various sorts unquestionably involves moral decisions but it suffers precisely because of its lack of a great unifying ethical principle, strongly and consciously asserted in society."[1]

[1] *Democratic Socialism,* p. 21.

Conservative liberals have thus found it necessary to turn to a standard of value which in some ways is very old, and yet which is perennially new, for it is a standard perpetually rediscovered under different names by persons seeking a serviceable and satisfactory mode of life. Plato and Aristotle laid down the principle that man's goal should be *eudaemonia,* which may be translated as *well-being.* A rounded and balanced well-being is implied—physical well-being, economic well-being, mental well-being, and spiritual well-being—the sort of happiness J. S. Mill was to call "the higher happiness," as opposed to the lower, more carnal pleasures. Mill's radical reinterpretation of Utilitarianism was in fact only a rather crude and awkward attempt to present the old theory of *eudaemonia* in modern dress. Perhaps the most satisfactory exposition of this doctrine is to be found in the writings of Edmund Burke. Burke gave it the rather curious name of "expediency"—implying thereby not material self-interest, but rather that self-interest which promotes the permanent well-being of the individual, the family, the social group, and the community as a whole.

Indeed, it is not only the right but the duty of each man to promote his own permanent well-being; but he must understand that his own permanent well-being can be secured only if he is careful always to maintain and advance the permanent well-being of others with whom he is associated. Similarly, it is not only the right but the duty of each social and political group, the state included, to promote both the permanent well-being of its members and of those of other groups.

It will be readily admitted that this statement concerning the rights and duties of the individual and of the state does not admit of rigid logico-empirical proof. Such a value system is not one of mathematical computation; it is not even capable of exact definition. We must, as Burke says, leave the understanding of its meaning "to the general sense of mankind"; and indeed it is the one value system which has proved satisfactory throughout history.

This value system is the basis both of Aristotle's dictum that it is the duty of the state "to promote the good life" and of the statement in the preamble of the American Constitution that it is the function of the government to "promote the general welfare." In fact, the two statements are really identical in meaning.

Conservative liberals readily accept the doctrine of *eudaemonia,* but in view of the aims of many statists, care must be taken not to misinterpret it. It is an essential part of the "permanent well-being" of each adult individual that he be, to use Mill's phrase, in large measure self-reliant and self-dependent; and it must be understood that any action of the state which seriously injures this self-reliance and self-dependence hurts rather than promotes the general welfare. It is the duty of the state to promote private and public morality, but nearly all attempts to enforce morality by police action end by weakening rather than strengthening observance of the moral code. When the followers of T. H. Green tell us it is the function of the state to promote morality by forcibly removing all temptations from its citizens, we can rely, in the wise words of John Milton, that a man is truly virtuous only when he deliberately and of his own free will chooses virtue, in spite of temptation. A man who is virtuous only because temptation has been removed from his path is not a saint but a puppet. We agree then that it is the function of the state to promote the public welfare, but it does not follow that men should be encouraged to live on hand-outs from the state, which lessen their spirit of self-reliance and demoralize their character.

It should also be borne in mind that neither the state

nor any other one social or political unit can or should have a monopoly of the function of promoting "the good life" or the general welfare. In accordance with Acton's dictum, when any one social or political group is given too much power, it will tend to abuse it; when the state alone is intrusted with promoting the good life, the result will not be an increase in the public welfare, but a gradual lapse into totalitarianism. "Promotion of the good life" is a function to be shared by a number of groups—by the state, of course, but also by the family and by various economic, religious, educational, social, and charitable organizations. And, as far as possible, participation in these organizations should be on a voluntary basis.

NATURAL LAW: A HIGHER AUTHORITY

Before quitting the problem of value judgments and their relation to political philosophy, it is necessary to examine the persistent problem of the existence or non-existence of what is commonly called "natural law."

From about 400 B.C. until about 1830 A.D. the great majority of political thinkers were convinced that there existed a law or a system of duties and obligations higher and more binding than any set of positive or man-made laws. In one form or another the idea of a higher law was accepted by Plato and Aristotle, and by many of the Greek dramatists; but since the beginning of the Christian era, largely because of the popularity of Cicero's formulation of Stoic ideas on the subject, it has been customary to call this higher law the "law of nature" or "natural law."

The doctrine of natural law, accepted and developed by the Christians, became an integral part of the scholastic philosophy of St. Thomas Aquinas in the thirteenth century and of the later scholastic writers, such as Bellarmine and Suarez in the sixteenth century. Belief in it survived the Reformation and long remained a basic part of political philosophy even in Protestant countries. Hooker and Grotius were its ardent advocates; it played a major role in the political philosophy of John Locke; and it was accepted without question in England by Burke, and in America by the radical Jefferson and by the conservative Federalists. Many of the decisions made by John Marshall while serving as Chief Justice of the Supreme Court were frankly based upon belief in the validity of natural law concepts.

To be sure the theory of natural law has long had its enemies as well as its defenders. In ancient times many of the Sophists contended that there is no objective standard of good and bad or just and unjust, and that hence there is no law that ought to be enforced irrespective of the wishes of the populace: the only valid laws are those invented by the arbitrary caprices of human groups, and these vary from time to time and from place to place. This doctrine in opposition to that of a higher law was taken over and popularized by the Epicureans and received a classic exposition in the great Latin poem *On the Nature of Things* by Lucretius shortly before the beginning of the Christian era. Driven underground during the Middle Ages, it reappeared with renewed vigor at the time of the Renaissance and was given forceful presentation in the writings of Machiavelli. But attacks on the theory of natural law were without conspicuous success until Bentham at the beginning of the nineteenth century launched his intense assault on the entire theory. This phase of Bentham's philosophy proved amazingly popular, and by 1850 there were few scholars or jurists in England or America willing to admit that there was such a thing as a higher or natural law. To most Anglo-American thinkers the only law that existed in actuality was man-made or positive law—the command of a sovereign enforced by sanctions.

Many of the outstanding political philosophers of France and Germany, however, continued to insist upon the existence and binding quality of some kind of higher law; and in the past few decades there has been a notable and rather startling resurgence of natural law concepts both in England and in America. This revival has been due in large measure to the failure of the legal positivists to provide a juristic basis for social and political organization which is satisfactory to man's innate instincts and attitudes. It now seems probable that a belief in natural law will again become dominant in the civilized world. It is certain the vast majority of the conservative liberals are convinced that the general acceptance of some sort of natural law concept is essential if civilization itself is to be preserved.

It is clear, however, that some of the older theories of natural law must be clarified and somewhat modified if the theory of "higher" law is again to win widespread acceptance. First, it is essential that some of the confused ideas popular in the eighteenth century be clarified and corrected. During this period many writers included under the term "natural law" both those laws that material objects *do* observe, and those laws which they felt human beings *should* observe. It is now obvious that the two concepts are quite separate and distinct, having little if anything in common. The formulation of generalizations regarding the behavior of material objects (or, if we prefer, the discovery of the laws of nature) is a matter best pursued by means of the logic-empirical method; but the formulation of codes on how man ought to behave requires the establishment of a standard of values—a problem on which the pure logico-empirical method gives us little help. Indeed there appears to be a flat contradiction between the way animals, including human beings, following "natural" impulses and in accordance with "natural" laws *do* behave, and how we feel that human beings *should* behave.

Secondly, the theory of the higher law must be rid of the loose ideas regarding the pre-political "state of nature" formulated by John Locke and others of his school. Locke held that before the formation of political units men lived in a condition of atomic isolation subject to no human law—a situation in which however, man was supposed to be both good and rational. Making use of his reason, man readily formulated or discovered "natural law," which by definition was nothing more than the dictates of right reason; and as all men had the same rational faculty, they invariably came out with the same answers. We now know that these ideas were based upon ignorance of man's early history. Man is a social or group-forming animal; and as far as we can discover, he has never lived in atomic isolation, but always in some sort of group which by its customary law exercises a rigid control over his actions. Furthermore, in early, primitive, savage days man was neither good nor rational but full of animal passions, and the art of reasoning was unknown to him. The doctrine of the higher law, knowable to some extent by reason, is not something which has come down to us from a pre-political period; it is rather a principle which was first fully and consciously formulated and recognized as man advanced towards civilization.

NATURAL LAW IN HISTORY AND PRE-HISTORY

We can, however, say that the rudiments out of which we were destined to develop the doctrine of the higher law existed in the earliest known times, even when man was living in a state of savagery. It would appear that at the very dawn of human existence man recognized that he could survive and prosper in his struggle with the forces of nature and with other animals only if he were in close and intimate contact with other men as members of a social group—which at first usually meant a group of his own kind. From the earliest times, therefore, there was not only a struggle for individual existence, but also close cooperation with others. In fact, there was only individual survival if there was also close group cooperation. Divided men fall, united men stand: though this adage was *felt* rather than understood, it served as the basis for the formulation and development of all socio-political groups. Without consciously reasoning about the matter, a man instinctively believed that in case of need he had a *right* to expect aid from other members of his group, both individually and collectively. This was the germ of the idea which later developed into the theory of "natural rights" and "natural duties" or "natural law." In later times when different kinship groups began to compete with one another, generally speaking that group which was the more coherent and compact, that group whose members felt the strongest call of "duty" to support one another, came out triumphant. It is not surprising then that eventually man became deeply imbued with the instinct of obligation to others, though for a long time this obligation was only to the other members of his own group.

In all cases these early kinship groups formulated elaborate codes of conduct binding upon all its members under pain of expulsion; and these codes became crystalized in the form of what is called customary law, which consciously or unconsciously had two ends in view. One was to preserve an iron discipline among its members, forcing them to speak, eat, dress and act alike in order to intensify the compactness and coherence of the group —a condition felt necessary if the group was to be successful in its struggle with other groups. The other aim was undoubtedly what we would now call the promotion of "the good life," or the promotion of "the well-being of the group and of its members"—though this aim was more instinctively felt than rationally thought out. If the group were to lead "a good life," it was necessary to promote the physical health or physical well-being of its members, and for this reason many primitive and semi-primitive customary laws contained strict injunctions (or tabus) about the eating or non-eating of foods which were thought rightly or wrongly to affect the health of its members. And since it was essential, if the group were going to lead "the good life," that its members should live in substantial harmony with one another, nearly all systems of customary law contained elaborate provisions concerning how different elements of the group were to behave to one another, how juniors were to behave to seniors, men to women, parents to children, and how descent was to be counted.

None of these codes of customary law was devised by a single individual; they developed, rather, over a long period of time and incorporated the ideas, feelings, and experiences of many generations. Nor were they formulated as the result of abstract reasoning on logical principles; they were rather the result of what the group elders, making use of what we may call unconscious as opposed to conscious reasoning, *sensed* would be for the good of the group. Looking over these codes objectively we can now say that at times these elders "sensed" wisely, and at others foolishly. For the most part, it was not their aims or ends that were wrong, but the means that they not infrequently chose to promote those ends.

Considering how radically the early kinship groups differed in environment, race, and accumulated experience, it is not surprising that many of these codes of customary law differ substantially on specific matters: certain foods which are permitted to be eaten by one group are prohibited by another; certain social or family relationships which are encouraged by one group are frowned upon elsewhere. What *is* surprising in view of the diversity of background is that so many of the codes of customary law are in substantial agreement on essentials, however much they disagree in detail. It is interesting to observe that in most cases, groups or tribes having codes of customary law similar to one another, and similar to what we may call the basic norm, are spread over wide areas of the earth; while groups which have what may be called peculiar and aberrant forms of customary law are generally to be found in isolated and more unfavorable areas—areas to which such groups have been pushed or driven back by triumphant enemies.

It would appear that even in the field of customary law there is a struggle for existence and survival of the fittest, and that in this field, at least, there is a tendency for the "fittest" to coincide with what we now call the "best." In other words, some codes of customary law proved more adequate than others in promoting "the good life" of the groups which obeyed them, and those groups which followed the more effective codes tended to triumph over those with less effective codes. It is among these effective codes that there is the greatest similarity, and so great is this similarity on most basic issues that from a comparative study it is possiible to construct a norm or generalzed code containing features common to all the more effective. In a general way we may say that the "well-being" of each group depended in no small measure upon the degree to which the cus-

tomary law of the group was in agreement with the norm
or generalized code.

In this norm or generalized code of customary law we
can see the germ of the "higher law"—but only the
germ, because among primitive and savage peoples we
never find any distinction made between (customary)
law as it is, and law as it ought to be. In fact virtually
every primitive group regards the customary code
which it has developed as being identical with law as it
ought to be. In a great many cases the belief in the identity of law as it is and law as it ought to be is fostered
and strengthened by the further belief that the customary law which the group follows has been given or revealed to it by the god or the gods the group worships.
To break or evade a law or custom, therefore, is not
merely to contravene the dictates of the group; it is also
to defy the god or gods who control men's fate.

Eventually, however, a time comes when some of the
members of some of the groups which have become large
and powerful are forced to question the identity of customary law with law as it ought to be. In the course of
historical development some small kinship groups develop into strong tribes whose domain extends over a
vast area, with the result that the spirit of kinship,
though not destroyed, is greatly weakened; and some
tribes further develop into those more elaborately organized social and political units which we now term
states. When this transformation takes place, there is
usually also a notable change in the social and economic
status of the people. Primitive nomadism gives way to a
life based upon agriculture. Commercial and industrial activity begin to appear, with a consequent ever
greater division of labor. Under such conditions, the old
code of customary law begins to lose its effectiveness and
its applicability to everyday life. Many of the provi-

sions of the law which in the old days had in fact helped to promote the good life are now felt to be "unfair" to certain individuals or groups of individuals. Thus in the Athens of the fifth century B.C., many men—and women—felt it advisable to break the traditional laws of the city state in order to fulfill obligations thought to be nobler and higher. We find a similar condition arising in the latter days of the Roman Republic. Originally the Romans were subject to a rather primitive type of customary law, later codified in the so-called Law of the Twelve Tables; but by the first century B.C. this set of laws had become anachronistic, and in practice the Romans were subject to a radical revision and reinterpretation of these laws incorporated in the Praetorian Edict, based upon the concept of the "law of equity and right reason" derived from the Stoic philosophy.

The need for a revision of traditional law codes in the light of higher, more generalized concepts of "fairness" and "justice" becomes especially obvious when, as has so often happened, one tribe succeeds in conquering and subjecting to its rule several other tribes. Under such conditions there is most likely to be a confusion and a weakening of the various systems of customary laws previously in vogue. Generally speaking, the conquering tribe tries to impose its traditional law upon the conquered peoples, but it is seldom that this attempt meets with complete success because the conquered peoples are unwilling and unable to adjust themselves to the legal concepts of the invaders. For a while the actual law in force is a special kind of positive law—the will of the conquering chiefs enforced by physical sanctions. In the long run, however, this sort of law generally proves unsatisfactory, even to the conquerors; and there gradually evolves a new system of law combining certain elements from the old traditional law codes of both the conquering and conquered peoples, but modified by and incorporating certain basic and generalized concepts of "fairness," or "justice," and "promoting the public welfare."

Thus we find that after Rome had conquered most of the Western world, the old Law of the Twelve Tables came to be completely forgotten, and in practice the Roman Empire came to be ruled by what was called the *Jus Gentium,* "the Law of the Nations," a system incorporating the salient features of the laws common to all the "nations" or tribes which the Romans had conquered, but also strongly tinctured with the abstract ideas of "justice" and "natural law" developed by the Stoics. This, and not the old Roman customary law, was the basis of what later came to be codified and termed Roman Law. The Stoic theory of "natural law" was to exert a strong influence upon all subsequent European jurisprudence, even the Common Law system of England which grew up outside the limits of Roman Law.

According to the Stoic theory, natural law is the dictate of right reason, and its content should be readily known to every rational being at any time or place. In other words every group of human beings reasoning about natural law should invariably come out with the same answers. We now know that this is not the case, for different peoples under different circumstances have come forward with divergent conclusions about the correct principles of morality and legality. At the same time this diversity of answers is often exaggerated. As was the case with the customary laws of the more successful primitive tribes, basically the ethico-legal norms developed by most of the peoples reaching a high level of material and social culture are remarkably similar. The norms evolved by Confucianism in China and by Buddhism in India are startlingly like those developed in

Europe under the influence of Stoic-Christian concepts, although these three systems developed quite independently.

We may also say that to the extent the norms of these three systems were crystalized into positive law enforcable and actually enforced by the state, they have actually aided in promoting "the good life" of the people. Where the systems differ from one another—and difference is mostly a matter of detail and emphasis—there is much to be said for and against the effectiveness and hence the "superiority" of each system, but it is probable that most modern observers of both East and West would accord the highest place to the Stoic-Christian. More than the other systems, it emphasizes the dignity and the worth of the individual, and most students of human relations have concluded that "the good life" can be effectively promoted only when this concept is steadily kept in mind.

ETHICO-LEGAL STANDARDS

In sum, the doctrine of the higher law in one form or another has played a vitally important role in the development of social and political relations since men emerged from the early tribal stage. Even those political philosophers in modern times who have most vigorously attacked the doctrine have in actuality accepted the basic idea upon which it is established. Jeremy Bentham, for example, was vehement in his assertion that there is no true law other than positive law—the commands of a sovereign enforced by sanctions; but he was equally vehement in asserting that a law is to be considered good or bad according to whether or not it promotes the greatest happiness of the greatest number—an assertion which of course postulates an ethico-legal norm upon which all laws should be based. Bentham's chief novelty lay in his claim that happiness or pleasure is the only thing to be taken into account, excluding equity and fair play as concepts necessary for the promotion of the good life. As we have already seen, his doctrine has led to very unsatisfactory results.

In like manner, Karl Marx violently denied the existence of such things as justice, morality, and the higher law. At the same time, he thundered like an Old Testament prophet against the injustices and inequities of bourgeois society, thereby unconsciously reaffirming the objective existence of the very things which he consciously denied. While the feeling that certain laws and institutions are "unfair" and "unjust" has done more to convert persons to Communism than the acceptance of the dogma of dialectic materialism, acceptance of Marx's ideas of what is fair and just has done more to increase human misery than the ethical norms of any other creed.

It is certain that at the present time the vast majority of men, consciously or unconsciously, do judge the goodness and badness of laws and of governments by some sort of ethico-legal standard, and it is equally certain that for the foreseeable future men will continue to do so. It is therefore obvious that the doctrine of the higher law, far from being outmoded, continues and will continue to play an important—nay, a vital role in political life.

Beyond question, the doctrine of the higher law will be a major factor in any attempt to maintain world-wide peace, both now and in the future. Because of the belligerency native to most men, it is hard to maintain peace between nations even at the best of times; it becomes doubly difficult if two nations or two groups of nations in close contact with one another are motivated by widely different ethico-legal norms. An historical example is provided by the troubles which arose when the European nations began to have close contact with the Chinese in the early part of the nineteenth century. Although the ethico-legal norms of the Europeans were similar in many respects to those followed by the Chinese, the differences were sufficiently great to arouse intense feeling on both sides when each side did, in perfect honesty, what the other side regarded as "unfair." For instance, in the famous Terranova case of the 1830's, the Chinese with their ethico-legal theory of group responsibilty felt they were behaving justly when they held the whole crew of a ship responsible for a crime committed by one member of the crew, while the Westerners (in this case, the Americans) with their theory of individual responsibility maintained that punishment should only be meted out to the person who had actually committed the crime. The accumulation of such misunderstandings between Chinese and Westerners eventually led to war.

An even more serious problem faces us at the present time. The Western or Free World and the Communist world have vastly different views concerning what is "right," "fair," and "just" in the conduct of international relations; and while this wide difference exists it is difficult to imagine any long-continued period of "peaceful coexistence." Certainly it will be difficult for an organization as the United Nations to function smoothly or effectively as long as its member states are unable to agree on what is ethically and legally right and wrong.

Even within the boundaries of any one state the general acceptance of a single ethico-legal norm is of utmost importance. There may be wide divergences with respect to sect and creed, and current political beliefs, and yet the state may remain strong and stable. But unless the vast majority of the inhabitants of a country are in general agreement on the broad principles of what is "just" and "fair," there is apt to be a serious weakening of all political ties, and the stability of the whole state is threatened. This need for common ground was recognized by Mill when he said that: "in all political societies which have had a durable existence, there has been some fixed point, something which men agree in holding sacred."[2] In most instances the "fixed point" which men have agreed in holding sacred has been an ethico-legal norm, some form of a belief in "natural law" which has been consciously or unconsciously adopted by all sections of the people.

In times past when the government was commonly in the hands of a king or an aristocrat, the kings and nobles on numerous occasions were restrained from acts of extreme tyranny by their acceptance of the idea that they should do nothing contrary to "natural law." At the present time when government by the majority is prevalent, the acceptance of the belief that even majority rule has its limits and the acts of the majority should be kept within the confines of "natural law" plays an important role in preventing coercion and persecution of minority groups.

It is clear, then, that a belief in "natural law" or "the higher law" continues to play an essential role in political and legal life. At the same time we must be careful not to carry the idea to extremes. We must beware of the idea so common in the eighteenth century that the use of abstract, deductive reason will provide a detailed code of natural law which can and should be transformed into positive law by the governments of

[2] "Coleridge" in *Dissertations,* vol. 2, p. 30.

each and every country as soon as circumstances permit. Many of the eighteenth-century philosophers maintained that natural law should include provisions for the means of acquiring and disposing of property, for the proper mode of conveyance by will and succession, and for laws regulating commercial contracts. The attempt to incorporate such matters into the higher law throws the whole idea into discredit.

Ultimately the higher law is based upon the *feeling* of the vast majority of mankind that social and political institutions ought to promote "the good life," and that the good life is possible only when governments and laws compel men to act "fairly" and "justly" to one another. On these two points general agreement can be reached with no great difficulty; but when we attempt to analyze which particular acts are "fair" or "unfair," marked divergences of opinion arise, because of the different traditions of particular nations and cultures. It is difficult, in turn, to reconcile or mediate between these traditions, since each of them is based upon the accumulated experience of many generations as to what specific legal arrangements do aid in promoting the good life. Abstract, deductive reasoning can play only a relatively minor role in solving this problem, though there is place for it in systematizing and clarifying the results of this accumulated experience, and in determining how the traditions of different areas can be synthesized into a larger, more comprehensive whole capable of being useful to an ever greater section of mankind.

In any case, political philosophy must regard natural law or the higher law as comprising not a multitude of rules but a few, simple, basic principles or norms in general accord with the moral code common to the great religions of the world. These few basic principles can and should be incorporated into the positive laws of each country, but this does not mean that each country should have the same set of positive laws, for the detailed application of a principle of natural law which proves useful at one time and place may prove useless and even harmful at another time and place under different conditions. To the extent that natural law is based upon such general concepts as the Golden Rule, or that men should be compelled to act fairly and justly to one another, we may say that natural law is eternal and immutable; but the detailed human laws which are derived from these principles are not only diverse but can and must be modified when a change in human conditions renders the observance of the old laws impossible or inappropriate.

NATURAL RIGHTS

We have seen that there is a continued validity and importance in the old doctrine of natural law. The same thing is true with regard to the old doctrine of natural rights which is only the doctrine of natural law in reverse. Natural law implies that each individual has certain obligations to his fellow citizens; natural rights imply that each man should be able to expect his fellow citizens to follow the same obligations in their treatment of him. It is obvious, therefore, that if we accept the doctrine of natural law we must also accept the doctrine of natural rights. But for the doctrine of natural rights to be of value, it too must be clarified, and rid of the erroneous concepts which grew up about it, especially during the seventeenth and eighteenth centuries.

Here again we must reject the old Lockean theory which saw natural rights originating in a mythical pre-political state of nature in which each man was completely free, being subject to no external control. We now know that there was no pre-political state of nature in the Lockean sense of the term, and that in very early times a man, far from being "free," was completely subject to the customary law of his kinship group, and that the only rights to which he could lay claim were those granted by customary law. At the same time it is clear that every system of customary law did grant to the individual member of the group certain rights, just as it imposed on him certain obligations. The specific rights accorded to the individual varied from group to group, but in all instances the rights granted were based upon the idea, or rather upon the feeling, that in order to promote "the good life" of the group as a whole, each member must be protected from arbitrary and "unfair" acts on the part of the others.

As civilization advanced and as social and political institutions became more complex, it was usually found necessary to reassert and redefine these rights in more specific and formal terms; and for this reason we can more easily recognize the particular "rights" accorded an individual in an advanced group than in a group living under more primitive conditions. In the numerous cases where a state or lesser political unity arose as the result of the conquest of one group by another, there was frequently a period when the conquerors acted ruthlessly and arbitrarily in their treatment of the members of the defeated group; but in time (and ordinarily sooner rather than later) it was realized that if the conquest were to be stabilized and if the state were to persist as an organized unit, it was necessary to accord to each person, even to the members of the conquered group or groups, certain well-recognized "rights" as safeguards against arbitrary and "unjust" treatment. History gives us many examples of this type of development. Only a few decades after the Romans conquered Gaul, they found it necessary to grant the Gauls many civil and political "rights." As a result most Gauls came to regard themselves as Romans. In like manner the Normans to prevent an uprising soon accorded the Saxons special guarantees against arbitrary treatment (i.e., "rights"), and in consequence the Normans and Saxons slowly but surely became blended into "Englishmen." In both cases, the establishment of a new, more complex political unity was accompanied by a definition of "rights" in more specific terms.

The particular rights granted to individuals varied from group to group in accordance with a diversity of ideas as to what "rights" were necessary to promote the good life; but there is remarkable similarity between the basic rights recognized both by many primitive and by most advanced groups. Nearly all law codes, both primitive and advanced, recognize the "right of life," or the right of each individual to be free from bodily injury by another member of the group or by the group as a whole, except in retaliation or punishment. The "right of liberty of action" is far less frequently recognized by primitive groups, for among most the minute details of a man's life are guided by customary law. But as human groups become more civilized and as division of labor becomes more general, the idea becomes accepted in legal codes that the well-being of the community and of each of its members is best promoted if the individual is granted a far-reaching "right" to do what he pleases and to say what he wishes so long as his actions and his words do not bring injury to others.

The "right of private ownership" or "right of property" is also a right which deepens and broadens as man progresses along the road to civilization. Among many primitive tribes we find a strong inclination towards socialist or pure communist principles, at least to the extent that the terrain inhabited or dominated by the tribe is held to be owned by the tribe as a whole and not by any individual member. Even among more developed peoples we sometimes discover, as in the case of the *allyus* (clans) of the ancient Incas or the *Mirs* (communities) of the ancient Slavs, that there is a certain amount of group ownership and operation of the land allotted to agriculture. Nevertheless, we find among almost all peoples, even the most primitive, at least the germ of the idea of personal property and property "rights"; and this idea also becomes more extended and more important with the development of the social and material culture of the people concerned. Among the most primitive peoples, though it is believed that the land as a whole belongs to the tribe, it is customary to recognize each tribesman's personal right to the fish or animal which he has caught by his own efforts, and each woman's personal right to the fruit or plant which she herself has gathered or tended, and to the pot which she herself has made. The idea that a man has a "right" to the product of his own labors is thus very ancient and almost universal. It is the development of this idea which led to the acceptance of more elaborate concepts of personal property rights in virtually all developed communities throughout the world.

The notion that a man has or ought to have certain intrinsic or "natural" rights is thus seen to be a concept existing in a germinal state among all human groups; but it is one which comes into full flower only when man approaches a fairly high level of civilization. Indeed, the increasing weight given to the idea of man's "natural" rights, or the rights which he *ought* to have, has been a major factor enabling certain communities to achieve high civilization. Here again it is well to point out the part played by the Confucian, the Buddhist, and the Stoic-Christian ethico-legal norms in the development of the idea of human rights. To be sure, neither

Confucianism nor Buddhism ever evolved a formal doctrine of "natural rights," but both systems, especially Buddhism, achieved almost the same end by emphasizing the dignity and worth of the individual and by insisting that the individual be protected against arbitrary interference from other persons and even from the community as a whole. However, the Stoic-Christian ideology gave the idea of individual rights its most rational and consistent development, and it was under the influence of this ideology that Roman law became the first of the legal systems to grant full recognition of the rights as well as the obligations of the *persona* or individual man.

The doctrine of natural rights is thus seen as an idea of great value in promoting "the good life." But history shows that at various times certain aberrations or misconceptions of this doctrine have led to an infinite amount of harm. One of these misconceptions is that natural rights can be divorced from natural duties or obligations. At the time of the French Revolution, for example, there were many persons who insisted they be granted their natural rights but were blind to the fact that in return for these rights it was necessary for them to carry out a corresponding set of obligations to their fellow citizens and to the community as a whole. Yet it is only when men are willing and able to carry out their obligations that they become worthy of being granted rights. A man has the "right" to life only so long as he respects the lives of others; the "right" to liberty of speech and action only so long as he is willing to curb his own speech and action to avoid injury to his fellow citizens and the community in which he lives; the "right" to private property only so long as the use which he makes of it does not injure or endanger the well-being of his neighbors.

Another serious misconception regarding natural

rights which tends to result in great harm is the notion that by the use of abstract, *a priori* reasoning we can construct an elaborate and detailed list of natural rights applicable to all times and places. We have seen that this idea is fallacious when applied to natural law; it is equally fallacious when applied to natural rights. The basic principle of natural rights is immutable insofar as this principle means each man possesses dignity and worth, and that as far as possible each man should be left free to promote his own well-being and that of his associates without arbitrary interference on the part of his fellow citizens or the state. But again it is necessary to insist that the detailed application of this principle will vary from time to time and from place to place, according to the intelligence, education, and moral character of the people concerned. This detailed application must also be in general accord with the accumulated experience of each national or ethnic group—with its manners, its customs and its traditions. Among the Anglo-Saxon people the right of trial by jury has mainly proved a useful and valuable application of the principle of natural rights; but among other peoples, who are unused and unprepared for this institution, the inauguration of the jury system would prove ill-advised and injurious. We are forced to reach the same conclusion with respect to many other concrete rights which some persons have insisted are "natural" rights, such as the right of universal suffrage.

A final misconception popular at the present time, especially among the more extreme radicals, is singularly liable to abuse. This is the theory that among the "natural" or "fundamental" rights which all people ought to enjoy is the *right* to a certain level of economic well-being, which must be guaranteed to them by the state. This idea has even been incorporated into some of the new national constitutions promulgated since World War II. The Japanese Constitution, for example, declares that the people have the right to live "free from fear and want"; that all people not only have the right to work, but shall also have the right "to maintain the minimum standards of wholesome and cultured living." We may well agree that the state should aim to improve the economic standards of the general population, but to claim that the people have a "right" to a given standard of living is apt to prove impractical and even dangerous—and contrary to the whole principle of rights properly understood. In many cases the application of these "rights" is possible only when a state has ample economic resources, and when it enforces some kind of population control so as to prevent these resources from being used up by an ever increasing number. Equally important is the fact that the whole theory of rights, when properly considered, is based upon the principle that on certain matters each individual should be free from arbitrary interference on the part of other individuals, or on the part of the state as a whole. In a properly ordered state such rights can and should be enforced by the courts of law. When, however, it is said that an individual has a "right" to a certain standard of living, it is difficult to see how such a right can be enforced by judicial proceedings. It is even more difficult to see how many of these rights can readily be implemented without such rigid economic and political controls as to form a totalitarian form of government, which is precisely what the theory of rights is trying to prevent. If the historic doctrine of individual rights is to mean anything at all, we must say that the state can and should promote the economic welfare of its citizens as far as possible, but only to the extent that this effort does not interfere with the basic rights of the individual.

[6]

Is There an Ideal Form of Government?

DEMOCRACY IS NOT ALWAYS THE IDEAL

WE ARE NOW in a position to examine the age-old problem—what, if any, is the ideal form of government? Shall we say with Carlyle that it is better for mankind to be ruled by the wise one or the wise few rather than by the ignorant many? Or shall we hold with Bentham that the only good form of government is one based upon universal suffrage and majority rule? Or, finally, shall we maintain with Montesquieu that no one system of government is suitable for universal application, and that we must conclude that that system of government is best which is most in accord with the manners, the modes of life, the traditions of the people concerned?

A careful study of history, ancient, modern, and contemporary, shows that the remarks of J. S. Mill on this subject are still of profound significance and value, even though developments since Mill's time make it necessary to modify some of his detailed conclusions. Mill was certainly right in supporting Montesquieu's position that no government is or can be effective unless it is in general accord with the character and spirit of the people as a whole at a particular time and place. Since different peoples continue to manifest quite divergent character and spirit, it is absurd to try to impose a uniform type of government upon all the countries of the world. On the other hand, Mill was equally right in insisting that when peoples do attain a certain economic, moral, and cultural level, certain forms of government are markedly superior to others, and that among the forms of government which must be considered superior are those which incorporate, in some form or another, the two basic principles of democracy and individualism. Due attention to the principle of democracy prevents the exploitation of the many by the few. Due attention to the principle of individualism prevents the exploitation of the few by the many.

Today, even more than in Mill's time, it is of the greatest importance to stress the truth of the first part of Mill's statement (derived of course from Montesquieu), that the ideal form of government must be in accord with the spirit of the people if it is to be effective. Because of the comparative success of democratic institutions in England and in America during the past century, many Englishmen and Americans have tended to forget or ignore Mill's dictum and have insisted that similar institutions should be imposed upon all the peoples of the earth, irrespective of their cultural or traditional backgrounds. Americans in particular are prone to take for granted that "the American way of life," including the American social, economic, and political pattern, can be taken over by all the peoples of the world without difficulty or danger. The events of the last few decades have shown the fallacy of this notion.

While congressional government has, on the whole, worked quite well in the United States, most of the attempts to establish similar forms of government in the

Latin American countries have met for many decades with very indifferent success (a fact predicted by so noted a radical as Thomas Jefferson). In recent years political conditions in many parts of Latin America have greatly improved, but it would be ridiculous to maintain that in the near future democratic institutions there will meet with no further difficulties. In like manner we may say that in England and in most of the British self-governing Dominions (above all those in which the bulk of the population is of British descent and has a common heritage of British tradition) parliamentary government has won the admiration of most competent observers. However, the attempt to establish similar types of governments during the prewar periods in France, in Italy, in Spain, and in Germany were far from being unqualified successes. In fact, the governments formed were so weak and so unstable as to invite the rise of dictatorships. It is greatly to be hoped that the newly reestablished democratic regimes in Italy and in Germany will meet with more enduring success, but it is certain that success can be achieved only if the German and Italian people have learned to adopt the psychological attitudes which alone make feasible the continued operation of democratic institutions.

The results of the many radical governmental changes in Asia in recent decades also illustrates very vividly the difficulty of establishing political institutions among peoples unfamiliar with them, more especially when such institutions run counter to the traditional *mores* and attitudes of the people generally. For more than two thousand years the Chinese were governed by political institutions in close accord with their own social customs and ideological background. These institutions were not perfect, but on the whole they worked well, as is shown by the willing acceptance of them by the vast majority of the people. During the latter part of the nineteenth century the *mores* and the basic ideas and standards of value of the Chinese were greatly altered, largely as the result of increased contact with the Europeans. With this change it became obvious that governmental institutions had to be somewhat altered and "Europeanized" if China were to remain well governed.

Competent students of Far Eastern affairs expressed the hope that these alterations or "reforms" would be made slowly and gradually, and that an attempt would be made to retain those governmental features which were still suited to the Chinese "psyche." Starting in 1906, the Imperial Court embarked upon a plan for political reforms in general accord with this idea. If this plan had been successfully carried out, the Chinese Empire would have been transformed into a constitutional monarchy within a few years, and there is good reason to suppose that this transformation would have resulted in a strong and stable government, eminently suited to China's need. But a group of radical "hot heads," most of whom had been educated abroad, and who had lost all contact with China's social and ideological heritage, were not content with this plan. They wanted not reform but revolution—a clean sweep of all existing Chinese laws and institutions; and they got what they wanted. The ancient monarchy went down in ruins and a Western-styled republic was established. In 1913 a new constitution was prepared which was little more than a Chinese paraphrase of the American constitution. Although China in her long history had never known a representative assembly or a popular election, even at the local level, she was now proclaimed a full-fledged democracy with universal manhood suffrage, and with a popularly elected president and a two-chambered legislative assembly.

The result was several decades of chaos. It was never possible to put the provisions of this first constitution into effective operation. While the government remained fairly stable as long as its first President, Yuan Shih-kai, acted as *de facto* dictator, after his death all semblance of law and order ceased. There followed a series of revolutions and counterrevolutions; and before long, most of the country fell into the hands of the various *tuchuns* or war lords. There was considerable improvement when the Kuomintang succeeded by armed force in securing control over a large section of China; but the Kuomintang frankly stated that the Chinese were not yet ready for complete democracy, and instituted a period of "tutelage." During this time control over the country was actually in the hands of a one-party dictatorship. In 1947 the Kuomintang proclaimed the period of "tutelage" over, and sought to inaugurate a new constitution, thoroughly democratic in character, but this new attempt to democratize China also proved premature. Exhausted by the problems resulting from internal dissension, inflation, maladministration, and civil and external war, the Kuomintang was vulnerable to attack. Taking advantage of this situation, the Communists were able to seize control of the Chinese mainland; and with this seizure, all hopes of democratizing China in the near future came to an end. In present-day China all power is in the hands of the Communist party which numbers less than one per cent of the population, and the Communist party is itself rigidly controled by a tiny group of self-perpetuating oligarchs. The "liberty" which the revolutionaries of 1911 so vigorously demanded—liberty of thought, of expression, and of action—is now completely dead.

We have dealt at length with the results of the attempt to democratize China at one fell blow, because we find here a classic example of the difficulties encountered in establishing governmental institutions alien to the traditions of a nation; but many other examples lie readily at hand. In recent years attempts have been made to democratize at a very rapid rate Egypt, Iran, Syria, and others of the predominantly Islamic lands; but apart from Lebanon, it is difficult to be well satisfied with the result. Many of these countries have witnessed the rise and fall of a series of inefficient and wasteful regimes. To maintain governmental law and order in Egypt and in Syria it has been found necessary to suppress, at least temporarily, parliamentary institutions and place power in the hands of a military junta. The governments of Jordan and Iraq have proved more stable, largely because the leaders of these countries have felt it advisable to preserve in greater measure some of the features of the traditional Islamic and Arabic heritage.

In Southeast Asia we find a similar situation. Since Burma established her independence in 1947, that country has been in a state of chaos. Five, and at times six, different "governments" have attempted to secure control by means of armed force, and though military action has now abated, the whole country seethes with dissatisfaction and unrest; the legally recognized government has still not been able to secure effective jurisdiction over the whole territory nominally subject to its dominion. The situation in Indonesia is just as bad, if not worse. Law and order have practically ceased to exist. A section of the population has lost all respect for the central government and engages in open lawlessness. Many of the army's territorial commanders operate as private war lords. It appears quite possible that the country will either lapse into complete anarchy or fall into the hands of dictatorship.

In some Asiatic countries, to be sure, where democratic institutions have been established, conditions appear to be much more favorable. Most agree that the new democratic governments of Turkey and of Japan are working rather well, largely because both countries were subject to a long period of tutelage in constitutional forms before control was handed over to the bulk of the people. Many observers also believe that the democratic institutions recently established in the Philippines and in India have a prospect of success. Certainly the fact that the Filipinos and the Hindus were introduced to democracy slowly and gradually and had experience with representative government long before they gained complete independence is a favorable portent. At the same time, there are other factors, especially with respect to India, which make it difficult to be overly optimistic. Apart from the top leaders, most Indian politicians have shown a distressing lack of public and political morality. Progress is handicapped by many age-old and deeply rooted superstitions; and it is difficult to see how democratic institutions can be successful over a long period when over 85 per cent of the population is illiterate. The test will come when Nehru and other present-day leaders, many of whom were trained in England and absorbed a great deal of the British tradition, pass from the scene, and India falls into the hands of new leaders who have come up from the ranks without this cultural background.

In recent years attempts have been made to establish Western-style democratic institutions among some of the Negro peoples of Africa, the foremost examples being the Gold Coast and Nigeria. As yet it is too early to give a final verdict on these experiments, but observers who have studied the situation at first hand are inclined to be pessimistic. The one area in which prospects appear to be fairly favorable is in that part of Northern Nigeria inhabited by the Hausa. Here the old tribal chiefs are still permitted to exercise some authority, and here the general population still shows some respect for traditional social and ethical codes—which is probably the reason that this area appears to be developing democratic institutions in an orderly fashion.

In our criticism of the achievements of democratic institutions outside of the countries which have inherited the Anglo-Saxon tradition, it should not be supposed that we accept the view that the Anglo-Saxon peoples are superior to the other peoples of the world, or that the successful operation of democratic institutions must be confined to peoples sharing the Anglo-Saxon heritage. In most respects the non-Anglo-Saxon peoples are the equals of the Anglo-Saxons, and in some respects their superiors. What *is* maintained is that because of their peculiar cultural background with its traditional reverence for the ideas of Milton and Locke, and Jefferson and the Federalists, the Anglo-Saxons have found it easier than peoples with a different cultural background to make effective use of democratic institutions during the course of the past century.

That successful operation of democratic institutions is not confined to Anglo-Saxons is clearly demonstrated by the fact that such institutions were functioning successfully in the Spanish states of Castile and Aragon many years before their adoption by the English. We must also recall that in the later Middle Ages such institutions as the États Généraux in France and the Landtage of many parts of Germany and Scandinavia also functioned very well. If they functioned well in the past, they can without question function well in the future, but only when they are once more in accord with the spirit, presuppositions, attitudes, and prejudices of the people concerned. In like manner it is certain that democratic institutions can be made to function smoothly among the peoples of Asia and Africa if, when, and as soon as a suitable transformation takes place in the psychologico-cultural background of the inhabitants of those continents. But until this time we of the democratic persuasion must refrain from insistence upon a democratic form as the ideal for all times, all places, and all peoples.

THE DIFFICULTIES OF DEMOCRACY

It must be borne in mind that though democratic institutions have functioned well in Anglo-Saxon countries during the last one hundred and fifty years, there have been failures as well as successes even here. A study of recent history should convince us that in Anglo-Saxon countries democratic institutions are neither fool-proof nor crook-proof. The study should also convince us that it is not invariably easy to maintain democratic institutions in all their purity when there is a marked change in the number, distribution, and character of the inhabitants of any one area. The enormous growth of the population as a whole, the great increase in the proportion living in congested urban areas, the constant incorporation into the community of persons of foreign birth and alien background, whatever may be the desirable by-products, have created difficulties in maintaining democratic institutions established when the countries had a small, predominantly rural population, sharing a common cultural background.

An examination of the operation of democratic institutions, both in Anglo-Saxon and non-Anglo-Saxon countries during the past century and a half, makes evident some of the difficulties which must be overcome if these institutions are to function successfully. In the first place, as Mill pointed out long ago, a democracy can survive only if most of the people genuinely desire it, and are willing to struggle, and if necessary fight, to maintain it. Even today many Germans and Japanese feel that democracy was forcibly imposed by the Occupation authorities and hence look upon it with suspicion and even resentment. If this attitude becomes widespread in Germany and Japan, democratic institutions there are inevitably doomed. But passive acquiescence is not enough. Democracy is always subject to attack by its enemies both on the extreme right and on the extreme left, and these attacks are often made so subtly that they are not easily detected. Eternal vigilance may be the price of liberty; but not even vigilance is enough. When attack threatens, the bulk of the people must be willing to counterattack vigorously and persistently. In addition to vigilance and aggressiveness, perspicacity is also a necessity. A large number of people, especially in France and Italy, claim to be intensely pro-democratic, and yet actively favor the establishment of a rigid and ruthless Communist dictatorship. This demonstrates none of the qualities necessary to insure genuinely democratic institutions, but rather leads to their overthrow.

Mill was also right in holding that a democracy can succeed only when most of the people are willing and able to carry out their responsibilities as voters. It is not sufficient for the people to claim the *right* to vote; it is also essential they realize that as voting citizens they have certain duties and obligations which they must be willing and able to shoulder. It is extremely difficult for citizens to cast their votes intelligently if they are completely illiterate. It is almost as difficult if the citizens, though literate, are ignorant of or are indifferent to basic national and international issues; and herein is encountered not only public apathy and problems of competition for attention, but also the as yet little analyzed aspects of "public relations," subtle propaganda, and covert censorship in all its phases.

It is difficult to maintain the successful operation of a democracy if a large portion of the population refuses or neglects to vote in public elections. It is even more difficult if a considerable percentage is willing to sell its vote, either physically or figuratively, to the highest bidder, and if the majority is willing to condone this and other forms of corruption, such as the intimidation of voters by threat of violence or by the stuffing of ballot boxes. Montesquieu was right in associating republics with "civic virtue," only to the extent of associating the success of republics with a high degree of such virtue on the part of population.

In addition to individual or private corruption, there is also the problem of public or mass corruption in the form of legislative, or executive, action giving special favors or financial subsidies to well-organized pressure groups, large and small, which are in a position to influence the results of elections. Often the influence of these groups is aimed directly at executive administrators of the government, by-passing both elections and elected officials, principally legislators. This type of corruption is by no means confined to democracies. Absolute monarchies frequently shower their favorites with gifts or grant them special privileges; and it is far from uncommon for aristocratic bodies to act in the same manner. The major democracies, however, are especially troubled by this problem because of the large number of persons and the immense amount of money involved. During normally good times, to be sure, the spokesmen for democracy, such as Bentham and Jefferson, ask for nothing more than equal opportunity for all and special privilege for none. All too often, however, professional politicians anxious to secure re-election are apt to pour public money into the hands of special groups exercising potential political power. In ancient Rome the Caesars secured and maintained dictatorial powers by bestowing free "bread and circuses" upon impoverished voters. In modern times such gifts usually take the form of "pork barrel" appropriations or large subsidies to specially privileged groups.

Recent history shows that democracies function successfully when most of the people are sincerely interested in the welfare of the country as a whole and are willing to subordinate, to some extent at least, special interests of class, geographic section, and religious sect. A widespread devotion to the general welfare is very beneficial to monarchies and aristocracies, but it is far more important in the case of democracies. For centuries the Chinese were noted for placing the interests of the family above the interests of the nation. This did no great harm so long as China was ruled by an all-powerful emperor, but it was disastrous when attempts were made to transform the nation into a democracy. For centuries India was noted for the profound hatred which existed between Hindus and Moslems; but this hatred was not deeply injurious so long as India was ruled by an autocracy. It developed into a serious matter when it became apparent in 1947 that India was to be transformed into an independent democracy. At this time it became clearly necessary to create two separate states, one predominantly Hindu, the other predominantly Moslem.

The bitter hatred existing between the classes in a number of European countries is one of the important factors working against the successful operation of democratic institutions. For this very reason, as Aristotle pointed out long ago, democracy encounters its greatest chance of success when a country has a large and powerful middle class which can serve as a buffer between upper and lower. Democratic principles remain strong in the United States in no small measure because of the fact that most Americans consider themselves members of the middle class. Finally, it is highly desirable, in fact essential, when marked class distinctions do exist, for the great bulk of the populace to believe in the existence of a "higher law" binding upon all classes alike and thus preventing the ruthless exploitation of one by another.

History also makes it clear that the functioning of democracy is severely handicapped when the citizens tend to place party and party interests above the welfare of the nation. Rousseau dreamed of a state completely without parties. We now know that this is a silly dream. In all modern states, certainly in all democracies, parties play a very important role in public and political life; and it is well this is so, because parties by cooperative efforts can accomplish many things isolated individuals can not. On the other hand, when party spirit and activity becomes so intense and so partisan as to override all other considerations, the welfare of the nation is endangered. Democratic institutions are also seriously handicapped when any one party becomes so strong by legal or illegal means that it secures monopolistic control over the state—especially if this control persists over a long period of time; for lengthy maintenance of power almost invariably produces corruption. Most observers are agreed that political life in the southern portion of the United States has been hurt by the long continuance of what is virtually a one-party system. They also agree that political life in the northern regions has been damaged by the growth of huge and powerful political "machines" nurtured by patronage. Such a machine is more often than not in the hands of a "boss" who quite commonly never holds office himself, but who can elect or defeat candidates and decide the fate of a great number of issues because of, among other things, the general apathy of the average citizen.

Equally injurious to the body politic is the development of "democratic centralism," a factor known in the United States but much more powerful in England. "Democratic centralism" means that all the members of a party, especially those who hold public office, are forced to support all proposals of their party—proposals which are usually formulated by a small group of party leaders. A Labor M.P. who gladly supports the Labor party program for agriculture feels obliged, in most cases, to accept willy-nilly, the Labor program for foreign policy, even though he personally violently dislikes it. The Tory M.P. all too frequently votes and speaks blindly as the party whip orders him, though he feels serious misgivings on some issues. When carried to extremes this principle leads to the blind obedience of party orders coming down from on high, with a resultant instituting of a "party discipline"—a characteristic of totalitarian regimes. This marks the death-knell of genuine democratic institutions.

History also shows that in many countries adopting democratic institutions a large section of the populace is more interested in the letter of the law or the constitution than in the manner the law or the constitution operates in actuality. In classical times Rome was transformed from a republic into an absolute monarchy without the vast majority of the Roman people being aware of this fact, because Augustus and his immediate successors took great care to preserve the old forms of republican government even after they had secured complete control over the state. Augustus demonstrated exceptional discernment in not assuming the hated title of "king" and assumed rather the military title of "Imperator" ("Generalissimo"); and speaking technically, during most of the years of his rule he was content to serve as one of the several tribunes elected by the people to protect their interests from the ruling oligarchy. The Senate continued to meet, and every year the consuls and other officials were elected; but in point of fact these legislators and officials were merely puppets in the hands of the all-powerful Caesars. A similar situation has arisen in modern states. In a number of Latin American countries a president has been able to make himself dictator without formally breaking any of the provisions of the nation's constitution.

Many persons, especially many Americans, are apt to regard the granting of universal suffrage as the best means of preventing the rise of dictatorship, but recent history shows that this idea is very far from being true. The Japanese were given universal manhood suffrage in 1925, yet this did not prevent the rise of Tojo's ruthless dictatorship in 1941. In fact, we know Tojo received the active support of the majority of the Japanese people as long as he was successful in his war efforts. The plebiscites carried out by Mussolini and Hitler were indeed shams, but virtually all competent observers agree that a large majority of the Italians and Germans genuinely favored their dictatorial leaders until these leaders met with military defeat. The confusion between the letter of the law and the way in which institutions actually function is not confined to the illiterate and the ignorant: Sidney and Beatrice Webb, although great scholars, were so carried away by a study of the provisions of the Soviet constitution they concluded that Communist Russia was a genuine democracy.

Finally it is necessary to note the sadly mistaken view of the early advocates of democracy who argued that with the establishment of democratic institutions the "people" would invariably elect the wisest and ablest persons to public office. Much as John Adams and Thomas Jefferson differed politically, they agreed that the citizenry of every nation was divided into two main classes—the one a large class constituting the bulk of the populace and consisting of ordinary run-of-the-mill persons, the other a small class which constituted a "natural aristocracy" composed of persons with superior character and ability. They also agreed that normally under a democratic system of government the ordinary citizens would follow the political leadership of the natural aristocrats and would tend to elect such persons to high office. In England, Bentham and James Mill, for all their radicalism, held very similar views.

Recent history shows these views to be hopelessly optimistic. It is equally wrong of course to assert that in a democracy the people will invariably elect the stupidest and the most incompetent to public office. In actuality, with universal suffrage different people at different times, following the prevailing mood or fashion of the moment, choose widely divergent types of persons to be their political leaders. At some times and places the general populace is delighted to choose as their representatives persons of distinguished ancestry, and possibly with inherited wealth and a polish and education well above the average. This was true to a large extent in the New England of John Adams' day and in Virginia at the time of Washington, Jefferson, and Madison (all of whom were "aristocrats," though with differing political opinions). It was true in some sections of England, especially in the rural areas during a large portion of the nineteenth century. In many an agrarian district the electors were happy to send as their representative in Parliament some lord's younger son who had just finished his education at Eton and Oxford, on the very ground that "he was every inch a gentleman" and hence in theory far superior to the ordinary man.

At other times and places substantially different standards and ideals prevail. Not infrequently it is essential to be born in a log cabin or its equivalent or at least "on the wrong side of the tracks" to be able to secure election to public office. The possession of private means, especially if the means are inherited, is regarded as a sign the candidate is an economic royalist and hence must be defeated at the polls. The fact that a man was educated at a private school or at a fashionable college means that he is ineligible for political life. The fact that a man has received little or no education, that he has scarcely ever opened a book, and that he speaks ungrammatically is sometimes an asset in politics rather than a liability. It is easy to point out other shifts in the vagaries of public opinion markedly influencing the outcome of elections. It is seldom that an ordained minister is elected to public office, but often the influence of the clergy is of great importance in deciding who does get elected. At other times and places a candidate has to be outspokenly anticlerical and irreligious to be sure of political success.

In periods of prolonged peace a military man usually finds no opening in politics; but after a successful war a prominent general tends to be a great political favorite. Sometimes the public demands public and private rectitude of its political leaders. At other times the electorate seems rather proud of the fact that its representatives are rakes and libertines, and even that they have been successful in acquiring huge sums of money by political manipulations. Not infrequently the close connection of a politician with a group of criminal gangsters and hoodlums is no barrier to continued reelection.

At times a man is elected to office as the result of long,

consistent, and eloquent advocacy of some political issue, but more commonly, particularly in the United States, a man is chosen because his views on many crucial issues are unknown—a fact which means he has made few political enemies. In the American presidential campaigns it is not infrequently "a dark horse" who wins both the nomination and the election. Closely associated with this phenomenon is the fact that in many democratic countries there is a marked tendency for some electoral districts to elect mediocrities to office. In such cases the successful candidate is neither outstandingly good nor exceedingly bad; he is capable of uttering a few banalities, but is not an eloquent speaker. There is not a trace of brilliance in him and hence he is regarded as "sound." Stanley Baldwin in England and Calvin Coolidge in the United States were examples of this type. They owed their success to the fact they seemed typical of "the common man" so dear to many electorates.

The desire of the ordinary citizen to see someone similar to himself in public office also leads to the selection of many candidates because of their ethnic origin. This is especially true in countries like the United States where there are numerous different ethnic groups. In many areas both the Republican and Democratic parties are forced to nominate a certain number of Irish, Italians, Poles, Jews, and Negroes for office, not because they are the best men available, but in order to win favor with special elements in the local population.

DEMOCRACY CAN BE THE IDEAL

It has been necessary to say a number of harsh things about the operation of the democratic process, even in those countries where democratic institutions have been outstandingly successful. Yet this is in no way meant to indicate we should turn our backs on democracy and seek some other form of government. In fact, when a people is willing and able to carry out the responsibilities which are necessary for the operation of democratic institutions, democracy is the highest and finest form of government. Democracies may and do have their inadequacies and defects, but these are less serious than those which characterize other forms of governments. Certainly the weaknesses of democracy are nothing compared with the horrible barbarities which inevitably result from dictatorship, whether the dictatorship is of the right or the left—whether it be imposed by the Fascists or the Communists. Indeed, the chief task of conservative liberals is to insure that democratic institutions are preserved in the face of the constant assaults of its enemies. Conservative liberals can and should attempt to eradicate some of the failings which appear in the functioning of democratic institutions, but in this attempt they must be exceedingly careful not to undermine the basic structure of democracy itself.

The best arguments in favor of democracy are those put forward by J. S. Mill over a century ago. Recent history has only confirmed their cogency and soundness. The first and most important of these arguments is the claim that "government for the people" can best be secured through the system of "government by the people." In other words, the common good or the general welfare can best be promoted when *all* sections of the community have a share in the government.

Bentham, insofar as he was right, supports this contention of Mill. Bentham was certainly wrong when he said that all men are invariably motivated solely by rational self-interest. For this reason he was equally wrong when he claimed that *all* kings are interested only in their own welfare and are oblivious to the welfare of their subjects; some absolute monarchs have been not only enlightened but also benevolent despots. Bentham was also wrong when he claimed that ruling aristocracies invariably govern in such a way as to promote their own interests and to injure the interests of the general populace; history produces several examples of dominant aristocracies well imbued with the spirit of *noblesse oblige,* which adopted a paternalistic attitude towards their subordinates and genuinely sought to protect their interests. But we must admit that Bentham was right to the extent there is a *tendency* in most men, when not controlled by religious motives or traditional standards of value, to place their own interest above the interest of other men, and even above the interests of the community as a whole. For this reason when any important element in the state has no voice in the selection of legislators or rulers, its interests are apt to be neglected. It is only in a democracy that every adult has a vote, and thus a voice in governmental matters; that every section of the community has a chance to influence legislation and thus see that its own interests are protected. Monarchies, aristocracies, and the various monolithic forms may and sometimes do govern wisely and well, but in general the interests of the small farmer, the petty tradesman, and the laborer are better safeguarded when they have a share in shaping governmental policies.

The other argument of Mill, though of lesser importance, is not without significance: democracy, when operating properly, has an important educational role in that it trains its citizen to shoulder the responsibilities of government. It teaches people by experience how they can best promote the common good through legislative and executive action. Even when men are dominated by motives of self-interest, this self-interest is not always wise or even rational. Until taught by experience in governing, the majority frequently make erroneous and sometimes disastrous decisions; but when the majority have to pay for their own mistakes (as they do under the democratic process), there is strong possibility that they will amend their errors and learn how to conduct government. Many observers claim the Philippine Islands in the twentieth century were better governed under American control than they are at present in the hands of the Filipino people themselves. Such observers also maintain that the inhabitants of India were better governed during the last decades of British rule than under the current independent regime. But even granted this be so, it does not of necessity follow that democracy in these two areas is doomed. It means rather that through lack of experience in shouldering political responsibility, the peoples of the Philippines and of India have quite naturally made serious mistakes. But there always exists the strong possibility that through longer experience in self-government the peoples of these two areas will eventually establish what will be universally considered models of good government.

Although democracy has its weaknesses and foibles (like all other forms of government), it also has its very strong side—a side so strong that some form of democratic control must play an integral and essential part in any governmental system which conservative liberals seek to establish and maintain. But if conservative liberals are true to their ideals, they must also see to it that democratic control does not mean the negation of the "rights" which they all believe that individuals and minority groups ought to possess and maintain. In the seventeenth and eighteenth centuries many political thinkers were naive enough to suppose that democracy and individualism *necessarily* go hand in hand, and this illusion persisted until the middle of the nineteenth century. It never occurred to such men as Locke, Jefferson, and Bentham that a majority when given political power would seek to harm any individual or any minority. They resolutely refused to believe that if the broad mass of the population, given the vote, they would seek by legislative means to expropriate the wealth of the well-to-do minority.

History of the past one hundred years shows that these men were mistaken. It is not true, of course, that a majority will always persecute a minority, any more than it is true that a minority will always seek to exploit a majority. This is clearly apparent in the fact that for several decades after given the suffrage the laboring classes of England and of America made little or no attempt to interfere with the property rights of the more fortunate few. But it is also true that in the long run there is a frequently recurring *tendency* for the many to take advantage of the few, just as there is a *tendency* for the few to exploit the many. For this reason the aim of those who are sincerely interested in establishing and maintaining a government directed at the promotion of the *common* good of the nation as a whole, as opposed to the special interests of the few or the many, must be to incorporate not only democracy but also individualism into the governmental process.

It must be admitted that combination of the two principles is not always easy to achieve. Many attempts to mitigate the potential dangers of unchecked majority rule have ended in failure. Mill, who felt keenly upon the subject, suggested that those persons with high educational qualifications and those persons who paid high taxes should be given one or more additional votes in order to counteract their numerical inferiority in relation to the general population. This system was in operation for many years in Belgium where it functioned reasonably well; but it was abolished on the demand of the laboring classes who disliked the granting of special political favors to persons outside of their own group, and it is extremely doubtful whether such a scheme would prove acceptable to any country possessing universal suffrage. Mill also proposed the principle of proportional representation in order to give a more adequate voice to special minorities. Theoretically this idea has much to recommend it, but inevitably it has resulted in practical failure. Certainly the special type of proportional representation tried at various times in Germany and France was disastrous. Most observers are agreed that the weakness and instability of Germany under the Weimar Constitution (1918-1933) and of France under the Fourth Republic was due in large measure to results of this system of balloting.

Sometimes the spirit and tradition of a people are sufficient to keep the actions of a majority in check. For a considerable period of time this has been true of England. For many years past the Crown has been completely impotent in political affairs, and since 1911 the House of Lords has been shorn of most of its powers. Consequently any political group which can secure, even temporarily, a majority in the House of Commons achieves control of the entire realm. There being no written constitution, no distinction is or can be made between ordinary legislation and fundamental or constitutional legislation. A majority of the House of Commons by simple legislative process can at any moment repeal all the safeguards of the individual incorporated in the historic Bill of Rights. Such a majority can expropriate all wealth in the hands of individuals and abolish *in toto* the principle of private property. To date, the traditional respect of Englishmen for the rights of the individual has kept the House of Commons in check. Even when the Labor party had a decisive majority in Commons a tendency towards moderation in legislation was present. Some industries were forcibly nationalized, but with compensation given to the owners. How long this moderation on the part of Labor will last is open to doubt; certainly if Aneurin Bevan and his group of radicals come to power, it is probable that traditional restraints will be swept aside.

Americans, certainly those interested in the preservation of individual rights, are pleased that the Founding Fathers provided an instrument of government which places a number of curbs upon the careless whims of temporary majorities. America to be sure is thoroughly democratic in the sense that universal suffrage exists, and in both federal and state governments all legislators are directly elected by the people. Nevertheless, as long as Amercians preserve and respect their written constitution there is restraint upon the actions of majorities which seek to undermine individual rights. Ordinary laws must be kept within the framework of the Constitution, as must all acts of executive officials. To be sure, the Constitution itself can be amended, but this requires the consent of specially large majorities, and ordinarily several years elapse before an amendment becomes operative, so that the public is less apt to be swept off its feet by the passing whim of the moment.

A great number of the countries which have established democratic regimes in the post-war years have also felt it necessary to protect individual and minority rights by the promulgation of a written constitution to which the actions of the ordinary legislative and executive agencies are subordinated. To carry out this object more effectively, express mention is usually made of the principle of judicial review, a process developed through historical processes in the United States.

The principles of check and balance and separation of powers were first promulgated by Europeans, but for some reason or other they almost never played any important role in European politics. In the eighteenth century England developed the parliamentary system in which the executive branch of the government was completely subordinated to the legislative branch; in fact the so-called executive branch became nothing more than a special committee appointed from its own members by the majority party of the lower house of the legislative assembly. The supposed check and balance between the upper and lower houses of the legislature also came in time to be almost meaningless, as in nearly all European countries the upper house, however selected, lost most of its power leaving the lower house in complete control of governmental affairs. The possible check and balance between the provincial and the national governments was seldom realized because very few European states adopted the federal system. The greatest number of these states, in their unitary form, had and still have a strong tendency towards the concentration of absolute authority in the national or central government with local governmental agencies relegated to unimportant roles. There can be little doubt that this circumstance, while not necessarily unfavorable to democracy, is indeed not conducive to the preservation of a healthy individualism, for individualism can best flourish when there is a serious rivalry between the different organs of the state, and no one organ is able to exert complete control over all sections of the community.

Is There An Ideal Form of Government?

It would be nonsensical to urge England and the other European countries to reject the governmental traditions which have evolved during the last century and a half. At the same time Americans, well satisfied with the preservation of a great portion of their own check and balance system provided by the Founding Fathers, look with regret upon the fact that a considerable number of the check-and-balance features have been weakened in recent years, and they feel effort should be made to restore the system in its entirety. There are, to be sure, numerous prominent persons who do not share this point of view, and in recent years a number have publicly stated that the United States would do well to adopt in whole or in part the English parliamentary system. But these persons have not fully realized that the check-and-balance and separation-of-power principles are the most satisfactory means of preventing the rise of arbitrary rule by a party or group which has secured temporary control over the lower house of the legislative assembly —especially if the country has a government which is highly centralized. In instances where the President is of one party and the Houses of Congress are controlled by an opposition party, inconveniences are bound to arise, but in such circumstances it is at least certain that neither party can exert absolute power. In like manner it is far from being a tragedy when the two Houses of Congress are controlled by different parties. It is also clear that if liberty is to be preserved, the judiciary must be kept free from control by either the executive or the legislative branch of the government. Last but not least, experience shows that it is imperative for the check and balance between the state and national governments to be preserved.

In sum, we may say that if democracy is the embodiment of the principle of equality, and if individualism is the embodiment of the principle of liberty, it becomes clear that to achieve the best possible form of government we must strive for a system in which equality and liberty are equally emphasized. To harmonize the two principles is not always easy. In fact they can be effectively coordinated only if there is a genuine feeling of fraternity or mutual good will between all sections of the community.

[7]

The Aim and Scope of the State

THE COMMON GOOD

FINALLY WE EMBARK upon a consideration of the all-important problem: (a) what is the true aim of the state, and (b) how can this aim best be carried out? The first part of the problem has already undergone considerable examination. Locke and the other extreme individualists held that the sole function of the state was to repel foreign invasion, to suppress disorder at home, and to punish crime. There are still many who support this point of view, but they are a small minority and for the moment this idea can be ignored, if only because of its lack of influence and popular appeal.

Bentham and his followers claimed that the true aim of the state was to do anything and everything which would promote the greatest happiness of the greatest number of the citizens. Even among those who supported this conclusion, however, there soon developed a sharp difference of opinion. Bentham, himself and the older Utilitarians asserted that the greatest happiness of the greatest number could most satisfactorily be promoted when the state maintained a strict laissez-faire policy and permitted each person to say and do what he pleased, both in the moral and economic sphere, as long as he did not injure any other person. Most of the later Utilitarians, the so-called Neo-Utilitarians, rejected this view and insisted that the greatest happiness of the greatest number is best promoted when the state exercises a great deal of control over the actions of its citizens. Later Utilitarianism thus led to collectivism and socialism.

Utilitarianism, in one form or another, still has a large and powerful group of adherents. But as we have already seen, an ever increasing number of people have become disillusioned with it, at least in its cruder aspects. They have learned, with J. S. Mill, that it is necessary to discard the numerical or arithmetical side of the "felicific calculus"; they have also learned that it is necessary to distinguish between the lower and the higher forms of pleasures. For this reason practically all conservative liberals aim not at the greatest happiness of the greatest number but at the greatest possible "good" or well-being of the community and above this of *all* sections of the community. But even this statement does not answer the question, how far can and should the state go in promoting the general welfare or the common good?

There are some who feel the state can best promote the common good by ignoring the desires and caprices of the individual, and compelling each person to do what he ought to do if both his own and the common good is to be advanced. Such persons argue that as ignorance and superstition are incompatible with the public welfare, the state must if necessary use force to dispel the ignorance and superstitious beliefs of its citizens. Such persons also claim that as widespread immorality damages the well-being of the community, the state must take peremptory measures to stamp out immorality. Finally, such persons insist that the common good in the economic sphere can best be promoted when the state exercises rigid control and regulation of every phase of commercial and industrial life.

Such a view is one sided, to say the least. A careful study of history shows that, generally speaking, a community attains a greater knowledge of truth and therefore increases in wisdom when the state steps aside and permits its citizens to form their own opinions after listening to the arguments advanced by all schools of thought, including those which are downright superstitious or silly. History also shows that most attempts to impose morality by legislation or by force have resulted in disaster, and that when a man is compelled to do certain acts and refrain from other acts as the result of state interference, he usually becomes less, rather than more virtuous. The state should indeed seek to promote morality, but it must learn that true morality exists, as Milton pointed out long ago, only when a man is free to choose between good and evil and voluntarily chooses the good. Finally, history shows that the general well-being of the community is best promoted, not when a large section of the populace is supported by government handouts or subsidies, but when each citizen tries as far as possible to be self-reliant and self-dependent. Certainly experience has demonstrated that the public welfare can best be maintained and augmented when due consideration is given to the principle of competition, and when superior industry and ability are given suitable rewards.

On the other hand it would be foolish to claim that the public good or well-being is always promoted by a policy of extreme individualism, under which the state is completely indifferent and inactive with respect to what its citizens think, say, or write; what they do in the sphere of public and private morals; or how they conduct their economic lives. In a word, the common good or the public welfare is best promoted neither by extreme collectivism nor by extreme individualism, but by a compromise which might be expressed in the phrase: "As much individualism as possible, but as much state interference as is necessary to maintain the common good." Generally speaking, the public welfare is best promoted by allowing each person to think, say, and do as he pleases; but when the expressions or acts, either moral or economic, of a person or group of persons threaten the general well-being of the community, it is not only the right but the duty of the state to interfere and put a stop to such expressions or acts.

The whole question of freedom and its limitations is so important that it is necessary to go into the matter in greater detail. First of all, it would be well to propose several general principles. One is that in order to come to a sound understanding of the proper relationship between the state and the individual it is necessary to reject completely the Rousseau or Hegelian theory of "freedom." Rousseau, it will be remembered, insisted that a man is free only when he does what is to his own real self-interest—in other words, only when he does what he *ought* to do. When a man does something because of a whim, a caprice, or a desire which is not to his true self-interest, he is no longer free but a slave; and if necessary, a man should be *forced* to be free. The Hegelians and the Neo-Hegelians adopted this theory and carried it to its logical conclusion: since, according to them, it is the state which knows what a man should do to advance his own true self-interest, the state should force a man to perform such actions, for only in this way can the state enable a man to be really "free." In actuality, this entire argument is a sophisticated plea for complete totalitarianism.

Once admitted as a valid basis for action, the Rousseau-Hegelian theory of freedom leads to state regulation and control of all human actions. Advocates of statism can well claim that a man is not truly free if he feels a liking for jazz or boogy-woogy: the state should compel him to be free by instilling in him a love of classical music. A man is not truly free if his caprices and desires lead him to frequent light musical comedies: the state in the sacred cause of freedom should force a man to do what he ought to do and compel him to attend performances of Shakespeare and the Greek tragedians. A man is not free but the slave of ignorance if he accepts some absurd religious dogma: the state in order to promote freedom should engage in some form of "brainwashing" to compel him to change his beliefs. On Hegelian principles, freedom of speech and press is not the ability to speak and write as one pleases or desires, but rather the freedom to say and to write what the state decides should be said and written.

All this is arrant nonsense. If a discussion regarding freedom versus compulsion is to have any serious meaning, we must define freedom as the ability of a man to say, write and do as he desires. True freedom is the ability of a man to perform certain actions even though these actions are *not* to his advantage. In some cases it may be necessary for the state to intervene and suppress certain actions on the grounds that they are incompatible with the well-being of others or with the general welfare, but we should be aware that such suppression is a limitation, though a necessary one, of freedom. This is the concept of freedom laid down by Milton and by Mill, the two greatest defenders of freedom. It is certainly the concept accepted by conservative liberals.

Another principle to be constantly borne in mind is that no system either of freedom or of compulsion, or any combination of the two, can be expected to bring about perfection in social and political life. Human nature being what it is, and human frailties being what they are, neither complete freedom nor complete compulsion can create Utopia. The most that can be hoped for is the slow improvement of the general standards of human existence. We can now see how foolish and naive were the eighteenth-century philosophers who proclaimed that all problems of human existence would be readily solved if each man simply were given complete and absolute freedom to act as he pleased. Observation of what takes place in collectivist and totalitarian regimes has now made evident the inaccuracies of the thinkers of the nineteenth and twentieth centuries who proclaimed the Kingdom of Heaven on earth if only men's actions were curbed and regulated by the state. We now know that as long as men are permitted to drink or not to drink as they please there will always be some drunkards, but we also know that rigid prohibition does not result in universal sobriety.

A third basic principle which must never be forgotten is that the amount of freedom which can safely be granted to an individual or group of individuals varies, and must vary, according to time and place and circumstances. It is impossible to say that all persons at all times and in all places must be given equal amounts of freedom. In times of peace and reasonable prosperity the state can safely allow commerce and industry to function with a minimum of control and regulation. In times of war and of great depression it may well be necessary to make this regulation and control much more stringent. In a country where the merchants and manufacturers are well organized and powerful and where employees and laborers are unorganized and weak, there is greater excuse for government regulation of conditions of employment than in a country where trade unions have become so potent that they can deal with management on equal terms. At a time when the railroads have a near-monopoly of the means of transportation, there is greater excuse for the state regulation of the operation of railroad companies than when railroads are in active competition with trucks, airplanes, and other forms of public transportation.

The same principle applies to the non-economic phases of public and private life. Normally the state should let a man decide for himself whether or not he needs medical attention, and whether he should go to an orthodox doctor, a chiropractor, or a Christian Science practitioner; but in face of an imminent epidemic, the state may well compel its citizens to submit to innoculation or other means of control of disease. Normally the state will do well not to try to enforce morality by legislation, but it has not only the right but the duty to step in if there is evidence of widespread activity on the part of criminal gangs engaged in white-slave or narcotic traffic. Experience has shown that attempts by the state to abolish the sale or consumption of alcoholic liquors to the public generally end in disaster, but experience also shows that it may be advisable to prohibit the sale of spiritous liquors to American Indians, most of whom seem incapable of consuming alcohol in moderation.

Generally the state should permit complete freedom of expression both in speech and in writing, but at certain times and places it is necessary to place curbs on this freedom. The wise statesman must always take into consideration the practical effect of unlimited freedom in this respect. Englishmen as a rule are remarkably phlegmatic and tend to be unmoved by vociferous agitators. For this reason the English government is not unwise in permitting Hyde Park rabble rousers to call upon their listeners to march on Buckingham Palace and hang the Queen. In Japan, on the other hand, the general public is much more emotional and much more easily aroused to action. An appeal by a Communist leader to a Japanese mob to march on the Imperial Palace and dispose of the Emperor might well lead to bloody riot. As long as this condition prevails in Japan, the police might well need to place some curbs on the freedom of expression. At the present time the general populace in India is even more excitable and susceptible to suggestion than are the Japanese. It is not surprising therefore that Nehru, though a true lover of liberty, has found it necessary to place a rather sharp check upon unlimited freedom of expression. As the character of the populace changes, these curbs can either be tightened or relaxed as circumstances demand. In sum, we can say that the true aim of the state is promotion of the common good, and that the best means of carrying out this aim is the adoption of what might be called a political philosophy of balanced freedom—an imperfect, non-Utopian freedom dictated neither by state compulsion nor by rampant individualism, but a constantly changing freedom in which these two elements exist in ever fluctuating proportions, determined by the needs and possibilities of the common good itself.

APPLIED FREEDOM

Having defined the true aim of the state, and having established a philosophy of balanced freedom as the means of achieving that aim, we can revise our ideas regarding freedom and then proceed to make application of the idea of balanced freedom in several specific areas.

Looking again at Milton, Locke, and Mill—all ardent advocates of freedom—in the light of the better knowledge of history and pre-history which we now possess it is evident that while much of what they said regarding freedom of thought and expression is still factually sound and logically valid, some of their statements require serious amendment. Thus the proposition put forth by Milton and by Locke that men in a pre-political state of nature possessed absolute freedom of thought and expression and that it was only in later times that selfish monarchs and designing priests attempted to institute censorship, is now known to be completely fallacious. We are now aware that in early pre-political times men were organized in kinship groups controlled by a very rigid system of customary law completely stultifying freedom of thought and expression, which in actuality was a matter of slow and gradual growth, with many periods of reaction.

Milton and Locke were also wrong in claiming that because the employment of force will not prevent the spread of ideas, the persecution of heretical ideas and their expression in speech and writing is useless. A hundred years ago J. S. Mill pointed out that history effectively demonstrates that persecution, if sufficiently severe, consistent, and long continued, can eradicate ideas repugnant to the state. The events of the past few decades confirm what Mill enunciated. Most persons agree that had the Nazi and Fascist regimes lasted several decades longer, they could have succeeded in eliminating most intellectual non-conformity within their domains. Most persons also agree that if the Communist regimes last another two or three generations, they will, by a combination of ruthless extermination and mass indoctrination, succeed in enforcing intellectual uniformity on their subjects. The success of some of the experiments in "brain washing" shows that in many cases the beliefs and ideas of men can be transformed in possibly less than a single generation, although recent events within the Soviet satellite states show that the extent of "necessary" severity and length is variable.

In addition Milton and Locke were optimistic, in fact naive, when they insisted that because all men are rational truth is bound to triumph when free discussion is permitted. Milton himself was to discover in later life that men are not always rational and that in forming beliefs and opinions they are swayed as much by passions and prejudices as by reason. In an open conflict between truth and error it is not always truth which conquers the minds of men, at least not at any one time and place. There are many instances when the broad masses of a country prefer to retain a belief in some absurd myth, even when the truth is repeatedly brought to their attention. Even in a cultured and educated nation there will always be some persons who will refuse to admit clearly demonstrated facts. In the United States there are thousands who still believe that the earth is flat and the sun revolves around the earth.

But though many of the earlier arguments in favor of freedom of thought and expression have now lost their validity, there still remains an overpowering argument in favor of this freedom. This argument, advanced with greatest clarity by Mill, in brief is that though freedom of discussion does not always eliminate error, it is only through free discussion extending over a long period of time, that truth can be discovered and made available to those who are willing to accept it. We cannot claim that the discovery and acceptance of truth always brings immediate pleasure (there are many unpleasant truths), but we can and must accept this principle: it is only through the discovery and general acceptance of truth that "the higher happiness" or the well-being of any people can be advanced. For this reason we must accept the doctrine that as a general rule the state should permit complete freedom of thought and expression.

However there are circumstances which require the state to make partial exception to this rule if the welfare of the community is to be safeguarded. As Walter Lippman very sagely remarks in his book *The Public Philosophy,* "Nobody can justify in principle much less in practice a claim that there exists an unrestricted right of anyone to utter anything he likes, at any time he chooses. There can, for example, be no right, as Mr. Justice Holmes said, to cry 'Fire' in a crowded theater. Nor is there a right to tell a customer that the glass beads are diamonds, or a voter that the opposition candidate for President is a Soviet Agent."[1]

The censorship of books and plays on moral grounds has always been a subject of much controversy. There have been many stupid censors, and attempts have been made to ban literary and dramatic works which were genuine works of art worthy of presentation before the public. At the same time there are limits in such matters, and the vast majority of people believe that the state should prohibit the public display and sale of literature which is outright pornographic and the public performance of plays which are openly obscene. In the case of the modern media of mass communication (press, radio, TV, and movies), there is a general feeling that there is an even greater need of censorship, as these media are apt to draw the attention of a larger, younger, more susceptible and less sophisticated audience. As far as possible it is preferable to allow the movie producers and the radio and TV stations to devise their own codes and boards of censorship, but the state must always reserve the right to step in if necessary.

In recent years a great deal of controversy has arisen

[1] *Public Philosophy,* p. 124.

as to the right or duty of the state to suppress opinions and movements which are clearly subversive, and which are aimed at the overthrow of free institutions. It is well known that both Fascist and Communist movements aim at the establishment of totalitarian regimes with the rigorous denial of all freedom of expression. The question is, Should nations which enjoy a wide range of freedom permit freedom of expression and activity to those who are trying to suppress this freedom? The problem is a complicated one not permitting of a simple and easy answer; but it is possible to lay down certain general principles.

In the first place, it should be remembered that all the great apostles for freedom of expression have put limitations upon the abuse of this freedom. Milton would not tolerate anyone's trying to undermine the foundations of the state. John Locke insisted that "no opinion contrary to human society or to those moral rules which are necessary to the preservation of civil society, are to be tolerated by the magistrates." Mill also felt that the liberal state is justified in curbing movements which threaten its whole existence and structure.

In this regard we currently find Lippman, a sane and moderate thinker, asserting that the right to use free institutions should be confined to those who adhere to them and wish to maintain them, and that it should be clearly understood that such counter-revolutionary movements as Fascism and Communism are enemies of the liberal state and should be suppressed. Sidney Hook has also recently drawn much needed attention to the distinction between heresy and conspiracy. The state can well ignore the speeches and writings of any one man, no matter how inane, heretical, or revolutionary; but when thousands of persons under rigid party discipline form an organized conspiracy to overthrow the free institutions of a state, the state has not only the right but the duty to see that the conspiracy is thwarted.

A sharp distinction should also be drawn here between private citizens and those who hold public office. In most cases the state can well ignore the opinions of private citizens however preposterous or outrageous—at least until these opinions have led to organized conspiracy. The holding of public office, however, is not a right but a privilege, and this privilege should be confined to those who are willing and able to serve their country wholeheartedly and competently. The state has the duty to dismiss those officials who are clearly loyalty risks or security risks, though it goes without saying that whether a particular person is or is not a loyalty or security risk should be decided by due process of law. No person should be dismissed merely because of wild and reckless accusations.

It is also a matter of some considerable importance whether an official's private beliefs are of such a nature as to permit him to function competently in his post. In the case of private citizens it is a matter of little or no significance if a man's religious beliefs cause him to utilize a form of faith healing in preference to the services of a doctor. In appointing a public health officer, however, it is well to ascertain whether the candidate is in general accord with the teachings of orthodox medicine. It is a matter of little importance if a private citizen is a sincere believer in the Gandhian doctrine of passive resistance, but it would be extremely unwise to appoint him to high office in the Defense Department. Again it is a matter of little significance if a particular man has peculiar and heretical views on the nature and function of law, but before confirming a man as a member of the Supreme Court, the Senate might well ascertain whether the candidate's legal philosophy is in general accord with the Anglo-Saxon legal tradition.

For the most part the American Army has wisely refrained from inquiring into the religious or political beliefs of its officers, but in instances where a commanding officer has views on tactics and strategy which lead to military disaster, he is quickly removed from his command. Where the opinions and ideas of a director of military intelligence have led him to formulate hopelessly erroneous estimates of the enemy's capabilities and intentions, he is quietly transferred to other duties, even though he was honest and sincere in holding those views. It might be well to follow more closely a similar course of action in other departments of the government. This is especially true of the State Department, which has charge of our relations with other countries. One of the principal duties of our foreign service officers is to prepare estimates of what other governments are likely to do or attempt. Occasional mistakes are inevitable and must be overlooked, but if because of private ideological quirks a diplomatic official consistently composes intelligence estimates which are highly erroneous, it would be patently advisable to transfer him to a post where his views are less likely to cause damage to our national interests. In practical application, freedom of thought and expression must not be made absolute, but limited according to a philosophy of balanced freedom.

ACADEMIC FREEDOM

Freedom of thought in the academic world is also a matter of balance. Beyond any shadow of doubt the general principle of academic freedom must remain the foundation stone of our educational system, especially with respect to state-supported educational institutions. In order to promote scientific advance it is essential that individual teachers and professors be permitted to advocate ideas which at the moment appear to be highly heretical, not only in the natural but also in the social sciences. No professor of economics ought to be discharged merely because he advocates free trade or a high tariff, or merely because he accepts or rejects the Keynesian theory of economics. No professor of political science should be dismissed merely because he defends or attacks the New Deal. But even with respect to academic freedom, it is necessary to draw certain limits. The American Association of Universities was undoubtedly wise in stating that any man who has become a member of the Communist party should not be appointed to an academic post, on the ground that a person who joins the Communist party automatically loses his freedom, being subject thereafter to strict party discipline not only with respect to his actions but also his opinions, and is thus incapable of conducting independent scientific research. Moreover if real academic freedom is to be preserved, it is essential that those who are members of any organized conspiracy to overthrow academic and all other forms of freedom should not be permitted to bore from within and thus undermine our free educational institutions. This is true whether the conspirators seek to establish either a left-wing or a right-wing form of totalitarianism.

Nor is it enough to exclude right- and left-wing totalitarians from the teaching profession in order to preserve academic freedom; it is also highly advisable to encourage the deliberate appointment of persons with diverse views to membership in large academic departments, especially in the field of the social sciences. A few decades ago it was sometimes possible for moderate right-wingers to exclude moderate left-wingers from professorships in certain universities. Such activities must be regarded as deplorable. But the reverse is likewise so. At the present time moderate or even radical left-wingers are in complete control of the social departments at many of our leading educational institutions, and it frequently happens that in such places it is quite impossible for conservatives, even those of very moderate persuasion, to secure appointments, or if appointed to secure further promotion. In a number of our colleges and universities, with all their talk of academic freedom, it is virtualy impossible for a non-Keynesian to be appointed to the economics department, or for a non-New Dealer to be appointed to the political science department.

If academic freedom is to be preserved, this freedom must work to protect moderate conservatives as well as moderate radicals. Educational institutions might well bear in mind the resolution passed by the Students for America: "Realizing that complete objectivity is impossible, we believe that there should be a reasonable balance of representative opinion in all departments dealing with political issues. As vacancies occur, we believe that every effort should be made to bring the composition of such departments more nearly in balance. This will enable the student to hear various points of view, so that in learning to weigh them, he may thereby gain maturity of judgment."

MORAL FREEDOM

The question of freedom of the individual in the moral sphere remains as yet unexamined. Conservative liberals, unlike some secularists and all Communists, do believe in an objective moral code—that some acts can be considered good and others bad. As they also believe that one of the principle functions of the state is to promote "the good life," it follows that the state should also seek to promote by education and in other ways the observance of this moral code as a necessary element in the good life. At the same time conservative liberals also reject the old Calvinist notion of state-enforced morality that everything which is immoral should also be made illegal. As both Milton and Mill pointed out, state-enforced morality is not morality at all, because when the state forces its citizens to perform certain acts it does not promote virtue but merely transforms these citizens into pawns and puppets.

Moreover, in many cases when the state seeks to enforce moral action by legal sanctions, the principal result is the promotion not of virtue but of hypocrisy. The citizens are outwardly virtuous but inwardly vicious. Not infrequently the chief result of attempting to enforce virtue is the growth of crime and corruption. The chief consequences of the Prohibition Acts was not to increase sobriety, but to foster warfare between various gangs seeking to control the illicit sources of alcoholic supply. Attempts to suppress all forms of gambling have often had the result of promoting large-scale syndicates willing and able to dispense huge sums to law enforcement officers for legal protection.

In general, therefore, we may well agree that the state should confine itself to the punishment of crime and of those acts which result in injury to others, leaving the enforcement of the moral code to public opinion and the social sanctions which result from the operation of public opinion. These sanctions are far from powerless. Legal sanctions do not prevent widespread drunkenness, but when "society" frowns upon an immoderate use of liquor men learn that it is to their advantage to refrain from overindulgence. Widespread social disapproval of sexual irregularities is a more powerful force in preserving the moral code than rigid laws.

With regard to freedom in the moral sphere, as on

other matters, however, we must seek to maintain balance, to avoid extremes. The state should not seek to punish acts merely because such acts are contrary to the accepted moral code, but the state must always be ready to step in and punish acts which threaten the moral well-being of the whole community. Thus we hold that the state should make a vigorous attempt to suppress the sale or use of narcotics, although at first sight it appears inconsistent with our contention that the state should not attempt to prevent the liquor trade.

This apparent inconsistency well illustrates both the application of the philosophy of balanced freedom and its definition in terms of the common good. In the first place everyone, except a few fanatics, will admit that the habitual use of narcotics is far more harmful than the habitual consumption of alcohol. Where the sale of alcoholic beverages is permitted there will invariably be a few drunkards, but the vast majority of the citizens will tend to be moderate, so that drinking will not seriously undermine health or character. On the other hand, there are few if any persons who are able to take to the use of drugs in moderation. A person addicted to cocaine or heroin soon becomes a physical, mental, and moral wreck, and the widespread use of narcotics in a country undermines its basic stamina and unifying fabric. For that reason, if for no other, the state should seek to suppress traffic in such drugs, extending "freedom" of use only for proper medical purposes and "compelling" non-usage for other reasons.

Secondly, the enforcement of prohibition laws is always difficult because of apathy on the part of a large section of the general public; and a great many people, in fact a very substantial minority, will simply refuse to obey the law. In addition, many who themselves give up drink will refuse to betray to authorities those known to be dealing with "bootleggers." With respect to the narcotics trade the difference is evident: in most countries the use of narcotics has spread to only a very small minority and is therefore much easier to check; moreover, the public horror of narcotics trade is so great that the average man is willing to give to the law enforcement authorities any information and help he is able.

In like manner, it can be said that while generally the state should not punish ordinary offenses against the sexual code, there are times and places where state action is necessary, especially where breaches of the sexual code have been placed on a large-scale and commercial basis. It would be foolish for the state to punish all cases of sexual irregularity, but it would be wise to punish persons who take profit from white-slave traffic. It would be foolish for the state to attempt to punish all who make a wager or who play at cards for a stake, but it would be wise to punish syndicates which make fortunes by securing monopoly of gambling facilities.

It is indeed absurd for the state to attempt to abolish drinking, gambling, and occasional sexual irregularity; for human nature being what it is, such attempts will fail. At the same time, it is well for the state to attempt to curb certain abuses which arise from drinking, gambling, and sexual activities. Not only has the state the duty to punish drunken drivers and those who sell alcohol to minors, but it may also limit the number of saloons permitted to operate in a given area and prescribe rigid rules on hours in which liquor may and may not be sold. While the attempt to abolish gambling is useless, the state may well lay down rules as to when, where, and under what conditions gambling may take place. It is impossible for the state to prevent occasional sexual irregularity, but it may well prohibit or regulate houses of prostitution. In all of these examples from the moral sphere, as in other areas of "freedom," individual freedom and state compulsion are in balance in different proportions, depending on an intelligent examination of the circumstances and the needs of the common good.

ECONOMIC FREEDOM

We now examine the exceedingly important problem of the extent to which the state should seek to control the economic activity of its citizens. Most of the violent disputes which currently take place in democratic countries center around the problem, and because of the extreme expressions of opinion which have been made and of the animosities which have been aroused, it is a matter of considerable difficulty to reach a reasonable and moderate conclusion.

In general it may be said that both the extreme individualists and the extreme collectivists have been faulty in their analysis of and proposed solutions to the problem. It is no longer possible to adopt the extreme individualism in economic affairs advocated by Locke, Jefferson, and Bentham. Bentham was at fault in holding that when each man worked for his own economic self-interest, he automatically advanced the economic interests of all other men. Some men, including both capitalists and labor leaders, work for their own economic self-interest in such a way as to cause serious injury to other men, and in these cases it is the duty of the state to prevent such action.

Bentham was also wrong when he claimed that all men act in strict accord with the demands of rational self-interest. Some men are so little rational that they do not and can not see what is in accord with their own self-interest. Other men can and do see what is to their self-interest, but because of laziness or moral weakness fail to do what they know they should do. In certain instances the state may well step in to protect a man from his own irrationality or moral weakness. All men know that they should save something for a rainy day or their old age, but many fail to do so. Consequently there is justification for the state to insist upon some form of compulsory saving, such as "social security," so that such persons will not become charges upon public charity when they are no longer able to earn a living.

Locke was certainly wrong when he maintained that the sole function of the state is to repel foreign invasion and punish domestic crime. The state must have some concern with the physical and economic well-being of its citizens. In times of great natural disasters, such as tidal waves, earthquakes, and floods, most persons agree that the state should take steps to ameliorate conditions. In like manner, when a nation suddenly faces economic disaster, it is the duty of the state to determine how the situation can be eased, and to provide some kind of relief for those persons who temporarily have no means of securing a livelihood.

Locke was also mistaken when he claimed that the state should be entirely unconcerned with the problem of how the total wealth of the nation is distributed. On this point Aristotle was much wiser; for while he was certainly no radical, he pointed out that a state is in an unhealthy condition when all or nearly all of a nation's wealth is concentrated in the hands of a few at the top, and the rest of the population is abysmally poor. Aristotle was also right when he declared that it is almost impossible to maintain constitutional government in a nation unless there is a large and powerful middle class, able to serve as a buffer between the more and the less affluent classes in society. It would be well for the modern state to keep in mind Aristotle's dictum.

Locke was assuredly in error when he claimed that the individual has not only a "natural" but also an absolute right to the private property he possesses. On this point, the ideas of Aquinas and other medieval philosophers have proved far more sound. The general principle of private property is indeed "natural" in man, and must be zealously safeguarded; but we must always remember that every right implies a corresponding duty, and this applies to property rights as well as to other types of rights. When a man grossly neglects the duties which go along with the ownership of property, he forfeits the rights to this property. A man does indeed have a natural right to liberty of personal action, but when he uses this right to inflict injury upon others, this liberty must be checked. Similarly, the right to property means that a man has a legitimate claim to the exclusive *use* of money, goods, or land which he has honestly earned or legally inherited, but this does not mean that he has the right to abuse or misuse this property in such a way as to cause injury to community in which he lives. If a man allows his land to become a breeding ground for malarial mosquitoes, if he allows his house to become a hiding place for rats infected with bubonic plague, or if he permits his cows to transmit tubercular bacteria, he cannot claim immunity from interference on the part of the state on the grounds that he has a right to do as he pleases with his own, for he has not carried out his obligations as a property owner. Hence the state can rightfully force him to amend his ways under threat of punishment or even confiscation.

But though the advocates of extreme individualism have often been guilty of serious error, the advocates of extreme collectivism have been even more fallacious. As we have already had occasion to observe, no non-dictatorial state can long endure unless there is a general acceptance of some sort of a "higher law" or moral code, binding upon all sections of the community. Any moral code, worthy of the name, includes a belief in "fair play" —the principle that no one element in the community should be in a position to take undue or unfair advantage of the other elements. The state should, therefore, require that the few rich do not exploit the many less-rich, but it should also see to it that the many less-affluent do not expropriate the capital of the well-to-do, most of whom have earned their money by toil and skill. Exploitation and expropriation are both contrary to the "higher law," and the state would do well to follow this principle.

The state must also bear in mind, when it seeks to regulate commerce and industry, that it is not omnipotent, that what it can and can not accomplish is frequently limited by the "laws" or empirical generalizations revealed to us by the natural and social sciences. When making elaborate plans to reorganize the economic structure of society, legislators would be wise to remember the maxims which can be learned from biology, anthropology, psychology, and economics; and Utopian dreamers should be reminded of the harsh facts of human nature, of human motivation, and of human compulsions which are to be gathered from these disciplines.

Take, for example, the problem of cooperation and competition. We should know from the social sciences that man is not always completely selfish. All men have some sense of altruism or cooperation, and with some men and some societies this feeling is highly developed. Society and the state should be prepared to take advantage of this fact. But it is also true that there is also a basic selfish strain in all men, and in many men, and in some societies this feeling is highly developed. It is this feeling which brings about competition. We must remember that we cannot eliminate this strain by education or legislation, and any scheme for economic collectivism which ignores this fact is destined to failure. Rather than try to abolish the feeling of self-interest and the principle of competition, the state should seek to harness these motivating forces so as to improve the community as a whole.

Competition takes many forms. Some men are more concerned with winning scholastic recognition, an elective office, or a medal than with receiving mercenary rewards. It is, however, beyond doubt that the desire for some kind of mercenary reward—the hope for a raise in pay, the desire to earn a little more than the other fellow—is a powerful motivating force with the vast majority of ordinary men. This desire for mercenary reward can and has brought about much evil; it also can and has brought about much good. The desire to secure more money has led to robbery and to murder. Where other social and political forces did not serve in a restraining capacity, it has led to ruthless exploitation of the mass of the society. At the same time, the search for profit in a competitive market has during the last two hundred years brought about an enormous growth of Western commerce and industry resulting in an astounding elevation of the standard of living of all sections of the population, including that of the common laborer. It has vastly increased the quality and the quantity of consumer goods and has brought the interplay of prices and wages to a point where material things are available to all elements of the population. The free market system is not perfect, but United States citizens now live better than the noblemen of former centuries and the nation is capable of dispensing its largesse all over the world. After World War II Germany made the most phenomenal recovery of any European country, largely because the Adenauer government had the courage to adopt the Erhard plan for the restoration of a competitive economy while the other countries made competition more difficult.

Mill was profoundly right when he stated that the opposite of competition is monopoly, and that any monopoly including governmental monopoly means stagnation, waste, and inefficiency. It is the duty of public opinion and of the state to see that economic competition is carried out fairly and honestly, and that there is no deceit and fraud. In the last century it was no doubt advisable for the state to try to prevent the exploitation of the laboring class by manufacturers through "Factory Acts" regulating hours and conditions of labor. With the growth in power and influence of the labor unions, however, most of such legislation has been rendered unnecessary. In most cases the working conditions in a given industry can best be left to the process of collective bargaining, which is really a special type of competition between management and labor.

If we accept competition as an essential element of our economy, it is also necessary to accept the principle of inequality of financial reward. If individual competition is to mean anything, a man who is willing to work a little longer, a little harder, and a little more expertly than his fellows should be entitled to a greater financial reward. In industrial competition a firm which produces goods of a better quality and at a lower cost is certainly entitled to a greater profit. We have already seen that when there is too great financial inequality among the citizens of a country, the results are unfortunate. But we must also accept the fact that an attempt to impose financial equality results in disaster. When all men receive the same reward, irrespective of the quantity, the quality, and the character of their work, economic decay is rapid and far reaching. When men are no longer motivated by the hope of greater economic reward, it is necessary to drive them with the whip of compulsion. Even Russian Communists have realized something of the truth of this principle, and in spite of their nominal egalitarianism have found it necessary to establish inequality of economic rewards. The pay of a laborer in Russia depends in large measure upon the quantity of goods he produces; and the salary of a factory foreman is many times that of the ordinary laborer. But the Russians still have much to learn: the long-continued failure of their agricultural program is largely the result of the Russian farmer's not receiving sufficient financial incentive to induce him to produce more ample food supplies; the more, and the less efficient farmers receive about the same rewards.

Even if we accept the premise that the primary function of the state is to aid in promoting the good life of its citizens, we must learn from repeated experience that the economic well-being of most of the people is best advanced by permitting and encouraging competition, subject to certain safeguards, rather than by allowing the state to assume direct control over the nation's economy. The reason for this is that generally speaking the average man as consumer can get more and better goods, and at a cheaper price, under a competitive market than when he is forced to purchase from a government-operated monopoly. We also discover the fact, seemingly paradoxial but certainly true, that in practice a free market economy tends to be more democratic in that it serves the needs of the greatest number of people more efficiently than the collectivist economy, which is presumably especially organized for the benefit of the majority. In a free market economy it is the people individually and collectively who by their choice in purchasing have a decisive influence on the nature, manner, and quantity of production. In a collectivist economy on the other hand, even in the one adopted by a democratic state, such matters are decided by an administrative bureaucracy often only remotely and indirectly controlled by the people. But if a free market economy is democratic (as the competitors have to appeal to the desires of the majority if they are to survive), it also leaves room for minority rights, as the minority also have a right in their choice of goods.

While in order to promote the general good it is wise for the state to recognize and make use of the competitive spirit, this does not mean that the state can or should have no regard for those who temporarily or permanently fail in the competitive struggle. In fact, it is the duty of the state to offer aid and assistance to persons financially handicapped because of natural calamities, or because they have been caught in the squeeze of a great depression. And some assistance should be given to those who have shown themselves incapable of fitting into the competitive world. This does not mean of course that the competitive system should be abolished just because it is wise and even necessary to grant aid to a few unfortunates. Above all, the state in granting aid to those in urgent need should bear in mind that its major aim in such cases is to rehabilitate the needy persons, so that they may once more at some future time become self-reliant and self-dependent.

Many persons who are ardent advocates of collectivism in economic affairs hold that it is an easy matter to combine economic collectivism with a rigid individualism in things non-economic, such as in the fields of thought, expression, and personal morals. It is highly doubtful this claim is valid. It is true that up to the present time most of the Fabian Socialists of England have made a sincere attempt to keep governmental regulation and control out of non-economic matters, but it is doubtful if this policy could be maintained once England were completely socialized. Certainly we know from recent history that most of the schools and parties which have been champions of economic collectivism have shown a strong tendency so to extend the collectivist principle to other spheres as to result in complete totalitarianism.

There are many differences in detail between the late Nazi–Fascist regimes of Germany, Italy, and Japan on the one hand and the present Communist regimes of Russia and China on the other; but they have one basic point in common: they all began with economic collectivism, and they all ended with states which completely regulated every sphere of human activity. Because of this strong tendency of collectivism to enlarge its boundaries, William Roepke was doubtless right when he stated: "It should really be no longer open to doubt that socialism goes hand in hand with a thoroughly authoritarian government. . . . In the long run economic dictatorship can as little exclude political and intellectual control as, conversely, political and intellectual dictatorship can exclude economic control. It is hardly conceivable naivete to believe that a state can be all powerful in the economic sphere without also being autocratic in the political and intellectual domain and vice versa."[2]

Many persons who have been ardent advocates of

---

[2] *The Social Crisis of Our Times.*

social and economic reform are now beginning to realize that the nationalization of industry is not the panacea they once imagined, and that nationalization of industry results in the transfer of property not to the workers but to a bureaucratic state. In a nationalized industry workers continue to be employees with all the regulation, discipline, and frustration of work under orders in large undertakings. Nationalization does not solve the problem of labor relations. It does not lead to higher wages. This being the case, we must look for genuine reform not through having the government take over the ownership and management of commerce and industry, but rather through trying to realize more perfectly the idea which Hilaire Belloc many years ago called the "Distributive State." Rather than trying to abolish private property, we should seek to broaden this institution and have it become more widespread "until free citizens are normally found to be possessors of land or capital or both."

The sense of ownership, which is the basis of private property, is a robust and deep-seated instinct. In an embryo form it is found among animals, for there are many animals which stake out an area as belonging to themselves and fiercely attack any intruder who dares to trespass. In a somewhat more developed form it has existed in almost every stage of human development. As society has progressed there has generally been a shift in emphasis from the collectively owned to the individually owned.

In many cases, this basic instinct, like many other fundamental human instincts, has led to abuses, and it is the duty of the state to punish these abuses and to prevent their recurrence; but it would be highly unwise to attempt to eliminate this instinct entirely. In fact the well-being of the community as a whole is enhanced when a very large section of the inhabitants are able to take advantage and make use of this human characteristic. There are still many imperfections in "the American Way of Life," but Americans should feel a sense of satisfaction that a very high proportion of their countrymen own their houses, possess automobiles and household gadgets, and have savings bonds and a few shares of stock —not infrequently in the company for which they work. It follows that those who would attempt to separate property and human rights, maintaining that the latter must be held above the former, are in error. Property rights and human rights are basic to each other; indeed a fundamental human right is the right of property and ownership.

Here we must bear in mind the truth of Mill's statement that in a well-run community "property" or capital is little more than the stored-up fruits of a man's own labor or the labor of his ancestors. In normal times in a country like the United States a man who is industrious and intelligent can receive for his services payment more than enough to meet current expenses. Some fritter away this surplus in personal indulgences. Others prefer to save this surplus. Eventually the money thus saved may become sufficient to use as investment, taking the form of purchase of materials, machinery, and human talent or labor, or of the bonds and stocks of large-scale industry. Because men are not equally industrious, intelligent, and skilled, and because some are more willing to save than others, it is ridiculous to advocate that all men should be restricted to the same amount of capital, as is the intent of certain forms of highly exaggerated graduated income taxation. The community is fortunate in which a large proportion of citizens are willing and able to satisfy their "ownership instincts" by acquiring amounts of capital in one form or another.

The Aim and Scope of the State

In general, therefore, it may be said that state ownership and operation of industry leads to far more harm
than good—even from the point of view of the laboring
man. But what about the problem of state regulation
and control? Everyone, with the exception of a small
number of extremists, willingly admits that *some* governmental regulation and control is necessary to protect
the community from injury resulting from the acts of
unscrupulous exploiters of other men's weakness and
stupidity. At the same time experience makes evident
that regulation and control should be kept to the minimum, because regulation at the very best is cumbersome
and unnecessary, and at its worst is decidedly deleterious
to the well-being of the community—as in cases in which
it leads to black marketeering or the decrease of production because of inhibiting red tape.

We have already seen that in the political sphere the
principle of check and balance is an important element
in the establishment and maintenance of good government. We may now say that the same principle of check
and balance is a very important element in maintaining
a sound economy, and that the principal role of the government in its regulation of the economy should be to
see that this system of check and balance does not break
down. Because of humanitarian principles or religious
and moral scruples there are many exceptions, but in
general when any group of people secure great economic
power they will tend to abuse it. For this reason, the
economic well-being of the community as a whole is best
served when the economic power of each group is
checked and curbed by the power and influence of other
groups. During a portion of the nineteenth century when
capital was strong and labor weak, capitalists tended to
exploit their employees. In recent decades, with the
growth of power of organized labor, often aided by gov-

ernmental legislation, the situation has been reversed. In many cases the trade unions have compelled employers to accept exceedingly severe terms, at times killing the goose that laid the golden eggs by causing industries to fail in the face of inability to meet the demands of labor. Generally the function of the government is to side neither with capital nor with labor, but to see that neither takes unfair advantage of the other, and to try to redress the balance of power when it fails to function properly.

We have spoken of check and balance between employers and employees, but this is only one phase of the conflict of economic interests in a modern community. Conflicts also exist between the different types of farming interests, merchandising interests, and servicing and professional interests; and it is the duty of the state not to give undue favors to any one of these interests, but to guarantee that none is able to secure monopolistic or even quasi-monopolistic power. In Europe many big industries in a special field have organized themselves into "cartels," in which all the major firms agree among themselves to keep production down and prices up. On the whole the influence of these cartels has been unfortunate in their effect upon the general or consumer public. The United States has wisely prevented the growth of cartels by a series of anti-trust acts aimed at maintaining genuine competition between the various firms in any one industry. These anti-trust laws have not always functioned without fault, but in general they have aided the public by fostering the increase of production and the lowering of prices.

Even in the United States the past several decades have witnessed the rise of great industrial and commercial combines. Certain industries such as steel, automobile, rubber, and tobacco are now dominated by a comparatively small number of firms, each of them of gigantic size. In some ways this development is to be regretted, though the result is not disastrous so long as genuine competition or balance is maintained. In fact the growth of these huge firms has had beneficial consequences, as Galbraith has pointed out in his brilliant book, *American Capitalism*. Among such beneficial consequences is the fact that the giant firms have been financially able, and indeed because of the competitive urge have felt compelled, to devote vast sums to scientific research and technological improvements, with ultimate benefit to the general public.

Galbraith has also conclusively shown that in many instances the growth of these giant corporations has brought about the development of a special kind of check and balance system, which he calls the "concept of countervailing power." In addition to the old competition between firms in the same industry, modern industrialism has brought about a new type of tug-of-war or competitive battle between different types of industries, more especially between large industrial firms on the one hand, and huge commercial corporations on the other. As an example of the check and balance between different types of industry we might cite the relationship between the steel and automobile industries. Steel production is now in the hands of a small number of giant corporations which can afford to neglect the demands of the small individual buyer; but they cannot ignore the demands of the huge automotive corporations for cheaper and better quality steel. As an example of check and balance (or countervailing power) between industrial corporations and commercial corporations, we may cite the many cases of large manufacturing firms forced to reduce their prices through the bargaining power of giant retailing organizations, such as the mail-order houses or the chain stores. For the most part this reduction has been passed on to the consumer.

Giant power becomes evil only when it is not in some way checked by other countervailing power of equal strength. When any one industry secures such power as to endanger the welfare of the community, the best thing that the government can do is not to seize or destroy it, but to permit or even foster the growth of other power which will be able to check and curb it.

BALANCED FREEDOM

We have spoken of the principle of competition, of check and balance, and of power and countervailing power. It would be of great advantage to the community if these principles were kept in mind in allocating the influence to be exercised by each of the main directive forces within the state. It has been said, and well said, that a community suffers when its ecclesiastical leaders have too great a control over its political rulers, or when its political rulers have too great a control over its ecclesiastical leaders. It might with equal justice be said that a community suffers when its political rulers exercise too great an influence over its economic affairs, or when its economic leaders exercise too great an influence over its political affairs. As ultimate guardian of the security and well-being of its citizens, the state must step in and curb the acts of any ecclesiastical organization which offers an open threat to the public welfare. In like manner, the state must intervene when any economic group (whether capital or labor) gets out of hand and endangers the common good. For the most part, however, the community is best served when spiritual, political, and economic affairs are kept in separate hands, and a healthy rivalry is maintained among the three. When all three, or even when any two, are controlled by a single group, we witness the decay of liberty and the rise of totalitarianism.

Finally, even when the state finds it necessary to interfere, it must do so not as a master but as servant; whenever the state allows any group, political or otherwise, to occupy too dominant a position, or whenever the state itself fails to respond to the needs of the common good, a vigorous public must itself intervene and make its wants known. But in making its wants known, even the public may not exert its power willfully, demanding the good of temporary majorities to the detriment of minorities, and freedom of action for some by means of arbitrary compulsion of others. Rather must the public, examining the particular circumstances with all the wisdom it can muster, exert its will in terms of the best possible good and the most possible freedom for all. Such wisdom implies, as we have indicated earlier, not only respect for the legitimate findings of science, but also respect for historical tradition, an informed knowledge of the basic nature of man and his world, and a proper understanding of natural law and rights.

So, at the last, we place the responsibility for good government in the hands of those to whom it belongs— the people themselves. The responsibility is a great one —one that is not borne easily, for the practical application of the political philosophy of balanced freedom, which alone makes good government possible, is a never-ending, ever-changing task, requiring energy, intelligence, and humility. But it is only thus that the great liberal goals of democracy and individualism, combined in whatever balance is at the moment most productive of the common good and individual freedom, can be achieved. Indeed, we cannot fully agree that that government which governs least, governs best; rather, that government governs best which *balances* best. The eternal search for that balance is a task to which free men— radicals and conservatives alike—can with dignity and pride devote their lives, their fortunes, and their sacred honors.

Suggested Readings

There are numerous books which deal with the problems discussed in this work. The following are some of the most significant.

I. For the partial-to-total disillusionment of modern radicals with extreme collectivism, especially see:

Crossman, R. H. (ed.). *New Fabian Essays.* London, 1952.

Crossman, R. H. (ed.). *The God That Failed.* New York, 1950.

Eastman, M. *Reflections on the Failure of Socialism.* New York, 1955.

Thomas, N. *Democratic Socialism—A New Appraisal.* New York, 1953.

II. For an exposition of views regarding the nature of the world and of man, especially see:

Boyd, W. C. *Genetics and the Races of Man.* Boston, 1950.

Dunn, L. C. and T. Dobhzansky, *Heredity, Race and Society.* New York, 1946.

East, E. M. *Heredity and Human Affairs.* New York, 1927.

Eddington, A. S. *The Nature of the Physical World.* Cambridge, 1928.

Jeans, J. *The Mysterious Universe*. New York, 1930.

du Nouy, L. *Human Destiny*. New York, 1947.

Pareto, V. *Mind and Society*. 4 vols. New York, 1935.

Walker, K. *Meaning and Purpose*. London, 1924.

III. For an exposition of various types of conservative liberalism, especially see:

Belloc, H. *The Servile State*. London, 1912.

Galbraith, J. K. *American Capitalism*. Boston, 1952.

Gilson, E. (ed.). *The Social Teachings of Leo XIII. New York,* 1954.

Hazlitt, H. *Economics in One Lesson*. New York, 1946.

Hogg, Q. *The Case for Conservatism*. London, 1947.

Hook, S. *Heresy Yes, Conspiracy, No*. New York, 1953.

de Jouvenal, B. *On Power*. New York, 1949.

Kirk, R. *The Conservative Mind*. Chicago, 1953.

Kirk, R. *A Program for Conservatives*. Chicago, 1954.

Lippman, W. *The Public Philosophy*. Boston, 1955.

Mosca, G. *The Ruling Class*. New York, 1939.

Roepke, W. *The Social Crisis of Our Times*. Chicago, 1950.

Rossiter, C. *Conservatism in America*. New York, 1955.

Ryan, J. A. and F. J. Boland. *Catholic Principles of Politics*. New York, 1948.

Wilson, F. *The Case for Conservatism*. Seattle, 1951.